"...A MAN OF STERLING WORTH
AND IRREPROACHABLE CHARACTER.
HE WAS PATRIOTIC IN THE FULLEST
SENSE OF THE WORD...."

A DESCRIPTION OF THOMAS J. HALSEY FROM
HISTORY OF THE ELEVENTH NEW JERSEY VOLUNTEERS,
BY THOMAS D. MARBAKER, SERGEANT, COMPANY E

Trailing hope and glory, the 7th New York Militia parades down Broadway on April 19, 1861, just days after the outbreak of war.

FIELD OF BATTLE

❖

The Civil War Letters of
Major Thomas J. Halsey

❖

By K. M. Kostyal

Prepared by the Book Division
National Geographic Society
Washington, D.C.

FIELD OF BATTLE

The Civil War Letters of Major Thomas J. Halsey

By K. M. Kostyal

PUBLISHED BY THE
NATIONAL GEOGRAPHIC SOCIETY

Gilbert M. Grosvenor,
President and Chairman of the Board

Nina D. Hoffman, *Senior Vice President*

PREPARED BY THE BOOK DIVISION

William R. Gray, *Vice President and Director*

Charles Kogod, *Assistant Director*

Barbara A. Payne, *Editorial Director*

STAFF FOR THIS BOOK

Barbara A. Payne, *Managing Editor*

Lyle Rosbotham,
Art Director

Victoria Garrett Jones,
Research Editor

Patricia A. Cassidy, *Illustrations Researcher*

Bonnie S. Lawrence, *Contributing Researcher*

Carl Mehler, *Map Editor*

Joseph F. Ochlak, *Map Researcher*

Martin S. Walz, *Map Production*

Barbara Brownell,
Concept Development and Contributing Editor

Martha C. Christian, *Contributing Editor*

Lewis R. Bassford, *Production Project Manager*

Richard S. Wain, *Production*

Jennifer L. Burke, *Illustrations Assistant*

Kevin G. Craig, Dale M. Herring, Esther Malo,
Peggy J. Oxford, Jennifer A. Serrano,
Staff Assistants

Karen Rice Gardiner,
Front Dust Jacket Design

MANUFACTURING AND QUALITY MANAGEMENT

George V. White, *Director*

John T. Dunn, *Associate Director*

Vincent P. Ryan, *Manager*

Anne Marie Houppert, *Indexer*

In a cold dawn reveille, a young drummer boy warms his hands.

About four million men fought in the Civil War, each of them battling more than the enemy. They worried about their families, about their own stamina and endurance, about courage and death, and about how much the war would ultimately cost them in spirit, health, or survival.

Thomas Jefferson Halsey was one of those four million. A devout man, he did all things faithfully—from serving his country to writing his wife. The letters he sent reflect one man's journey through the war, from the early optimistic days of his soldiering life to the hellish trials of Chancellorsville, Petersburg, and imprisonment in South Carolina.

Halsey's letters have been passed down through his family for four generations. Through the generosity of his great-grandson William and great-great-granddaughter Megan, they now appear here. To make the letters more accessible to a modern reader, liberties have been taken with punctuation and paragraphing, but Halsey's spelling has been retained. The letters have been excerpted to present the most relevant passages and the most compelling picture of Halsey. The accompanying text gives details on life in the field, on battles, and on the politics and mores of the time.

A New Jersey railroad man and farmer, Thomas Jefferson Halsey—"Jeff," as he calls himself in his letters—was nearly 36 when, in August 1862, he was mustered into service as a captain in the 11th New Jersey Volunteers. Most men in his regiment were friends and neighbors from Morris County, and they soon found themselves part of the Army of the Potomac, stationed on the outskirts of the nation's capital.

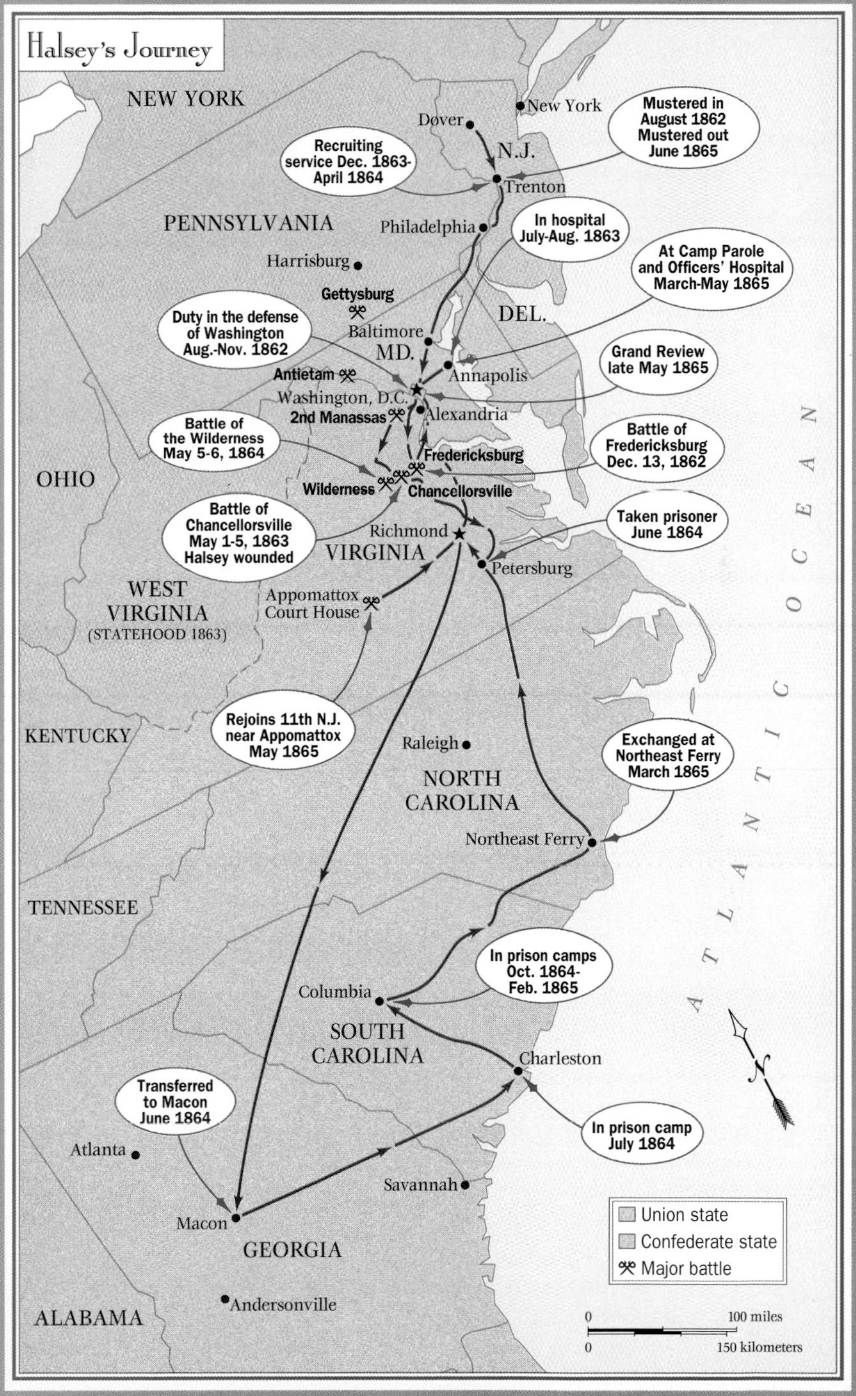
Halsey's Journey
NEW YORK
PENNSYLVANIA
OHIO
WEST VIRGINIA
(STATEHOOD 1863)
KENTUCKY
TENNESSEE
VIRGINIA
NORTH CAROLINA
SOUTH CAROLINA
GEORGIA
ALABAMA
N.J.
MD.
DEL.
ATLANTIC OCEAN
Dover
New York
Trenton
Philadelphia
Harrisburg
Gettysburg
Baltimore
Annapolis
Antietam
Washington, D.C.
2nd Manassas
Alexandria
Fredericksburg
Wilderness
Chancellorsville
Richmond
Petersburg
Appomattox Court House
Raleigh
Northeast Ferry
Columbia
Charleston
Atlanta
Savannah
Macon
Andersonville
Mustered in August 1862 Mustered out June 1865
Recruiting service Dec. 1863-April 1864
In hospital July-Aug. 1863
At Camp Parole and Officers' Hospital March-May 1865
Duty in the defense of Washington Aug.-Nov. 1862
Grand Review late May 1865
Battle of the Wilderness May 5-6, 1864
Battle of Fredericksburg Dec. 13, 1862
Battle of Chancellorsville May 1-5, 1863 Halsey wounded
Taken prisoner June 1864
Rejoins 11th N.J. near Appomattox May 1865
Exchanged at Northeast Ferry March 1865
In prison camps Oct. 1864-Feb. 1865
Transferred to Macon June 1864
In prison camp July 1864
Union state
Confederate state
Major battle
0 100 miles
0 150 kilometers

Left at home with five children—Burt, Ella, Frank, Elmer, and Thomas—Halsey's wife "Lib," Sarah Elizabeth, relied on their farm and allotments from his army pay to support her until his return. Like many Northerners, the Halseys anticipated a quick end to the war. But the war took on a life of its own and for almost three years consumed their lives. "I fear the war will not soon end," Halsey wrote his wife. "...How I wish it might be closed with honor and that our beloved land might once more be united and happy...."

In 1861 the United States was little more than an untested concept. The fragile, fractious union of states had functioned together under a mutual Constitution for less than a hundred years. In the course of those years, the two halves of the country—North and South—had moved in vastly different directions. By the mid-19th century, the North had embraced the new age of industry, its factories and cities attracting a large immigrant population, its mesh of railroads webbing it into a mighty whole. Much of the South, on the other hand, clung to the romance of Jeffersonian agrarianism—to an idyllic provincial life of farm and family, ordained, in the words of Mississippi's Reuben Davis, as the "primary pursuit of man." Davis must have meant white man, for the South's idyll survived on the backs of millions of slaves, most owned by an elite class of planters at the pinnacle of Southern society. These planters held sway in class-conscious antebellum society, particularly in the Deep South. Sent North to Washington as Democratic congressmen and senators, they launched long rhetorical battles in the Capitol chambers, defending and extolling slavery.

The opening of western lands only exacerbated the rift between free-soil Northerners and slave-power Southerners. For a while, the government tried to maintain an impartial balance, admitting one slave state for each free state. But the uneasy peace could not be kept by mere legislation. In the countryside, the dam was slowly giving way. An abolitionist zealot named John Brown was waging his own bloody raids and retaliations against pro-slavery factions in the Kansas Territory. By 1859 he had devised a grander scheme and moved his war

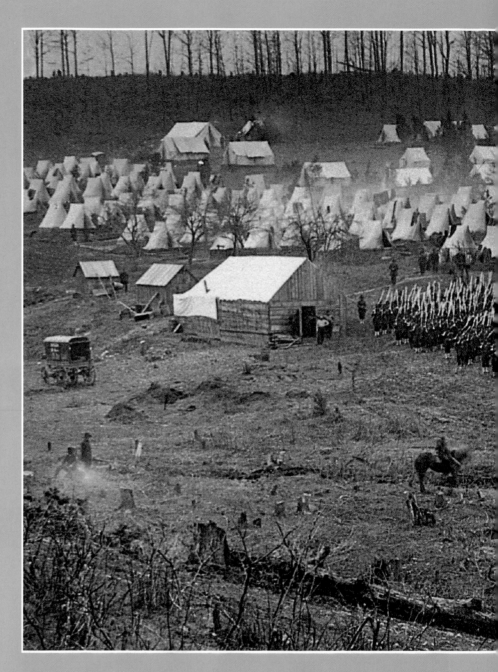

east, to a small town with a Federal arsenal: Harper's Ferry, Virginia. In October, Brown and his raiders grabbed the armory and held it for a day before Federal troops under Lt. Col. Robert E. Lee overwhelmed them. "When I strike," Brown had said prophetically, "the bees will begin to swarm." He was right. The South believed Brown's vigilantism

was just the beginning of a mounting Northern threat to its very existence. William Seward, then a congressman from New York and later Lincoln's secretary of state, warned that the nation faced "an irrepressible conflict between opposing and enduring forces."

With the elections of 1860, the irrepressible conflict could be

Perfect regimental rows line a hillside at Camp Northumberland near Washington in 1861. Such early pictures celebrated regiments at their full might, before war ravaged them.

repressed no longer. Abraham Lincoln, a dark horse Republican with an antislavery reputation, was elected President; six weeks later South Carolinians did as they had threatened to do: They seceded from the Union. The other cotton states—Alabama, Florida, Mississippi, Georgia, Louisiana, and Texas —soon followed. But Lincoln, com-

mitted to the preservation of the Union, refused to acknowledge the rights of states to secede. On April 12, 1861, the first shots were fired at Fort Sumter, a Federal fortress off the coast of Charleston. By June Virginia, Arkansas, North Carolina, and Tennessee had followed their Southern brethren out of the Union. A new nation, the Confederate

States of America, announced itself, eventually establishing its capital as Richmond, Virginia, about a hundred miles south of the Federal capital of Washington, D.C.

For the South the war took on "the sanctity of a religious cause," Georgia poet Sidney Lanier wrote. For the North it seemed, in those early months, a preposterous insurrection to be put down quickly and easily. To that end Lincoln called up an army of 90-day volunteers in April. As the 90 days dwindled and political pressure mounted, he ordered his commander, Gen. Irvin McDowell, to attack the Confederate stronghold of Manassas Junction, a railroad depot 29 miles southwest of Washington. On July 21, McDowell complied, knowing his army was far from ready. "You are green," Lincoln admitted, "but they are green also."

Eager to enjoy the sport, Washingtonians rode out to the countryside to watch the Northern army stampede the upstart South. But the battle did not proceed so neatly. Though the Yankees seemed destined for victory, the situation reversed itself in midday, with Brig. Gen. Thomas J. Jackson's Rebel brigade refusing to yield the high ground. The moment took on immortality when Confederate Brig. Gen. Barnard Bee yelled to his own men, "There stands Jackson like a stone wall! Rally behind the Virginians!" By day's end the "easy Yankee victory" had ended in defeat. Soon after, Lincoln began what would become a years-long search for a general to beat the South in the East.

In the western theater,

Lincoln had more hope. Already the opposing sides were facing off over control of the critical border states and central waterways. In Tennessee, a little-known commander named Ulysses S. Grant had proved himself a tenacious fighter against the Confederates at Fort Donelson in February 1862 and again at Shiloh in April—though the 24,000 casualties there had appalled the divided nation.

Hoping for similar victories in the East, Lincoln put his trust in Maj. Gen. George McClellan, a

glamorous and popular figure whom the press likened to a "Little Napoleon." After repeated urging, McClellan at last swung into action in the early spring of 1862. Landing 100,000 troops at Union-held Fort Monroe, Virginia, on the mouth of the Chesapeake Bay, McClellan began his Peninsula Campaign, planning to march northwest to Richmond. But at Yorktown he was waylaid by the Confederates' indomitable Gen. Joseph E. Johnston. It was late May before McClellan reached Richmond's outskirts,

United States Before Secession ❖ 1860

BRITISH NORTH AMERICA

WASHINGTON TERRITORY

OREGON

UTAH TERRITORY

CALIF.

NEW MEXICO TERRITORY

PUBLIC LAND STRIP

UNORGA-NIZED TERR.

NEBRASKA TERRITORY

KANSAS TERRITORY

INDIAN TERRITORY

TEXAS

MINN.

WIS.

IOWA

MO.

ARK.

LA.

MICHIGAN

ILL. IND. OHIO

KY.

TENN.

MISS. ALA. GA.

VT.
N.H.
N.Y. MASS.
R.I.
PA. CONN.
N.J. DEL.
MD. WASHINGTON, D.C.
VA.

MAINE

N.C.

S.C.

FLA.

MEXICO

Free state
Slave state
Territory

0   600 miles
0   900 kilometers

and there Johnston attacked again, sustaining serious injuries himself. Jefferson Davis replaced him with Robert E. Lee. A former officer in the U.S. military, Lee had garnered such a reputation for leadership before the war that Lincoln had offered him command of the Northern army. But Lee, a native Virginian, had refused.

While McClellan hesitated, afraid his forces were outnumbered, Lee—an engineer by training—had his men dig earthworks to fortify Richmond. And he called for reinforcements from "Stonewall" Jackson, who had been waging his brilliant Valley Campaign in the Shenandoah. Using the gaps and ridges in the surrounding mountains, Jackson and his 18,500 men had managed to occupy twice that many Federal troops, keeping them away from Richmond. Now Jackson hurried to Lee's aid.

In the Seven Days' Battles that commenced in late June, Lee saved Richmond, though at a high cost in casualties. Still, he had proved himself an audacious foe. When McClellan withdrew north, Lee soon followed. For the next year, the fighting would center mostly in Northern Virginia.

Saber-wielding Gen. P. G. T. Beauregard urges his Confederates forward at First Manassas. The Rebel victory here in July 1861 stunned the North, giving rise to the realization that a brutal, protracted war might lie ahead.

CAMP SEWARD
AUGUST 28, 1862

My Dear Wife,

...I am on my trunk under a peach tree on Arlington Heights in sight of the City of Washington and camps of thousands of men in every direction. Hundreds of waggons & horses by thousands. This is War on a grand scale....

Our regiment was ordered to report ourselves to G. B. McClellan at Alexandria. I can assure you there was great commotion in our camp. The Boys recieved the news with a shout ready for a fight with anything that came along....

We remain set under marching orders. The teams are still here but the Col. thinks we may stay here some time. We can hear the roar of canon...all along the lines and it is amusing to hear the camp rumors. The Boys have the Rebles within eight miles of us quite often and I confess that they are as near as I care to have them, but we shall soon be ready for them....

It makes my heart sad to think of what is yet to come. What must it be when there are a million of men in hostill array. The thought is sickning. I hope it may grow better and that this fair herritage may be transmitted to our children as we recieved it from our Fathers....

Your affectionate and loving husband,

Countryside of Manassas, 29 miles southwest of Washington, saw battle twice in just over a year. In this scene of the Union's Second Manassas debacle, Gen. John Pope's bluecoats fight to stave off Stonewall Jackson's advancing Rebels. Battle casualties: 14,000 Union, 8,400 Confederate.

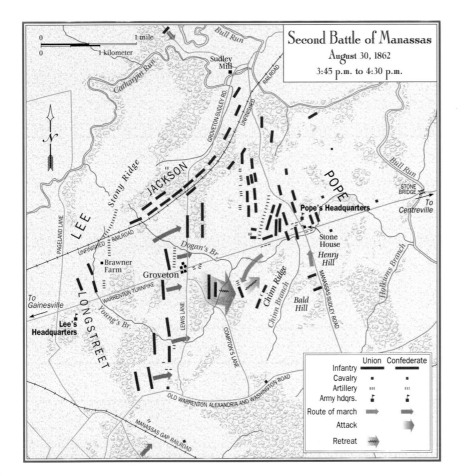

Second Battle of Manassas
August 30, 1862
3:45 p.m. to 4:30 p.m.

	Union	Confederate
Infantry		
Cavalry		
Artillery		
Army hdqrs.		
Route of march		
Attack		
Retreat		

With the failure of McClellan's Peninsula Campaign, Lincoln had formed a new Army of Virginia, commanded by the pugnacious and deeply disliked Gen. John Pope. So vitriolic were Pope's statements that even the equanimous Lee referred to him as the "miscreant."

By August, Pope and Lee were in a face-off in northern Virginia, and McClellan's troops were moving up from Richmond to add to the Northern might. Knowing this, Lee acted with what would become his trademark boldness. Dividing his army, he sent Stonewall Jackson's men on a flanking maneuver around Pope. Two days and some 60 miles later, Jackson and his men were feasting on supplies at Pope's Manassas Junction supply depot. Learning of this, Pope ordered his forces to "bag" Stonewall. With Pope thus preoccupied, Lee, reinforced by Maj. Gen. James Longstreet's wing, moved up to join Jackson's right flank.

On August 29, Second Manassas (called Bull Run in the North) began as Jackson's Stonewall Brigade held off Pope's attack. The next day, Pope ordered his men to pursue what he mistakenly believed were the retreating Confederates. Jackson's men, joined by Longstreet's, forced the Federals back to Chinn Ridge. By nightfall the Union was in retreat, retracing the course it had followed at First Manassas, 13 months earlier.

SPRING-SUMMER 1862

❖ **March - August** McClellan attempts Peninsula Campaign on Richmond, which ends in failure.

❖ **April 6 - 7** Battle of Shiloh takes place. Union claims victory.

❖ **April 16** Confederate Congress enacts conscription.

FRIDAY MORNING
AUGUST 29, 1862

Wife,

I finished last night what I had to say and laid down to take a knap. I had been asleep about three hours when I heard the Col. at the next tent. I hurried out when he told me to have the men hurried out with their arms for a hurried march, that there was a guerrila raid expected in this neighborhood and we and the other regts. in this vicinity must go to meet them.... My being Officer of the Day, I could not go with my Company. I am sorry, for if they have a brush with the Enemy I want to be along, but I think it will all end in smoke.

I have been out this morning looking about and find that the woods have been cut down for miles in every direction, so that we have a most splendid view of the surrounding county, Washington five miles distant with the Potomac between and some five or six forts to be seen. It is a most grand sight.

Yours as ever,

...One of the greatest essentials to a soldier's comfort in winter was day by day becoming more scarce—that was, an ample supply of fuel. It required from a hundred and fifty to two hundred fires to a regiment for the purpose of warmth and cooking. This number, multiplied by the number of regiments in a brigade, division and corps, called for the consumption of a vast quantity of wood, and forests near an encampment disappeared as if by magic.

FROM *HISTORY OF THE ELEVENTH NEW JERSEY VOLUNTEERS*

As spring arrives, the Army of the Potomac abandons its winter camp at Falmouth, Virginia, leaving deforested desolation in its wake.

Feeding the fires of a company kitchen required vast amounts of wood.

The opposing armies of the Civil War wreaked as much havoc on the landscapes they moved through as they did on one another. The camp and kitchen fires needed to feed and warm thousands of men voraciously claimed huge amounts of wood, and forests were leveled overnight.

When the cold weather set in, the armies typically gave up the fight and went into semipermanent winter quarters until spring came and the roads and weather made war possible again. In these vast winter camps, the men would often "log up" the sides of their tents or build simple huts for warmth. All of that ate up more woodland, as did the corduroys—roads and paths of logs—built to avoid the endless mud made of wet winter ground by passing wagons, horses, and thousands of feet. Men detailed to woodcutting might have to venture several miles from camp before they found any standing forests. Then they would return with a sizable wagon train full of logs to keep the camp supplied.

Water, too, was a prized commodity, and water parties often had to march some distance to find anything potable—or they made do with whatever water was available. With thousands of men and horses using the same streams, they soon became sullied, but with no alternative men drank even "warm, muddy, and stagnant fluid that had accumulated in some hollow."

SUMMER 1862

❖ **June** David G. Farragut's ships begin Union attack of Vicksburg, Mississippi.

❖ **July 1** Congress approves federal income tax to fund war effort.

❖ **Late July** Plans begin for the Confederate invasion of Kentucky.

Dear Wife,

...We have been expecting an attack from the enemy but I think the danger is passed and it may yet be some time before we have a brush with the enemy. I like soldiering full as well as I expected. It keeps my mind constantly employed and my health and appetite being good, I make out to pass the time quite pleasantly. But after all, Lib, I miss my quiet home, the prattle of my children and the companionship of a loving wife. But duty called me in the service of my country, and I feel that I ought to be here....

Yours ever,

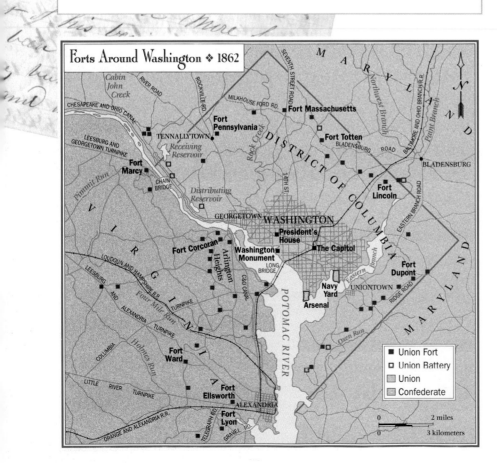

Forts Around Washington ❖ 1862

The war caught Washington unprepared in every way. Virtually undefended, the capital city was surrounded by hostile factions—Southern sympathizers in Maryland and the outright enemy just across the Potomac River in Virginia. In the first weeks after the fall of Fort Sumter, volunteer regiments en route to the capital from the North were greeted by rock-throwing mobs as they passed through nearby Baltimore, and pro-Southern partisans burned railroad bridges

Formidable defenses of Fort Totten, on the capital's northeast perimeter, include a Parrott gun capable of hurtling shells six miles.

and cut telegraph wires, isolating the Federal city. But as new volunteer troops poured into Washington, their sheer numbers soon guaranteed its safety.

In late May, Federal forces moved across the river, securing the nearby Virginia port of Alexandria and the high ground of Arlington Heights. Still, the capital could claim only one outmoded fortress in its defense—Fort Washington—and that lay 11 miles down the Potomac. The War Department did not com-

pletely recognize Washington's precarious position until after the Union upset at First Manassas. Unbelievably, the enemy had routed the Federal forces—and just a scant 29 miles from Washington's doorstep. A mad torrent of fortress building in and around the capital ensued. Eventually 68 forts and batteries rimmed the city, forming a 34-mile defensive perimeter. But even with that, the enemy came calling—just once, in 1864— at Washington's door.

SUMMER 1862

❖ **August 4** Lincoln issues a second call to the states for 300,000 more militiamen after his first call on July 2 failed to produce the required numbers.

❖ **September 2** Pope is replaced by McClellan as head of the Union Army defending Washington.

IN CAMP NEAR FORT LYON
SEPTEMBER 8, 1862

Dear Wife,

...hard march yesterday 16 miles through the dust & the sun shone very hot.... Drinking strange water does not have a very good effect on our bowells.... Yesterday, as we were marching along, I happened to look at my watch & thought of Sunday School then in and you in your quiet home.... I wish you would retain my letters. I shall want them as a journal when I get home. I had to borrow this paper....

Yours affectionately,

Disease carriers, canteens were filled with whatever water came to hand. Unless water looked or smelled objectionable, men assumed it was safe to drink.

Near Fredericksburg, soldiers gather around a stewpot. Generally, the men took few precautions in how or what they ate, and disease spread quickly.

The men who fought in the Civil War were felled more often by disease than by enemy fire, with twice as many soldiers dying from illness than from battle. At the time little was known of how diseases spread or the part that sanitation played in health, so camps were breeding grounds for illnesses. Men from rural areas, who had had less exposure to certain viruses and bacteria, were hit hardest. Mumps, measles, and diphtheria swept through armies, but the real killers were fever, typhoid and malarial; dysentery and diarrhea, often caused by bad water; and lung ailments. Together, these accounted for more than half of the Union deaths by disease.

"One of the wonders of these times was the army cough...," a Union soldier recalled of the winter of 1862-63. "When one hundred thousand men began to stir at reveille, the sound of their coughing would drown that of the beating drums."

Scurvy also plagued the troops. Although the Union added desiccated vegetable cakes to the army rations as an antiscorbutic, the men found the "*desecrated* vegetables" unpalatable. To them the greatest enemies were the insidious "graybacks"—lice. One writer reported that "the minds of the soldiers were exercised with far greater activity in planning campaigns against the *pediculus,* than...against Lee."

SUMMER 1862

❖ **September 4-5** Lee's army begins crossing the Potomac into Maryland, beginning his first invasion of the North.

❖ **September 13** Union soldiers inadvertently discover a copy of Lee's invasion plans wrapped around three cigars; McClellan proceeds with plans to circumvent Lee.

Dear Wife,

...I now realise what it is to be away from home and the surrounding of friends. And may God in his Providence grant that this fratracidal and terrible war may soon cease. I am in hopes that this last desperate effort of the Rebels may teach them that they never can invade the North with any chance of success. If matters have turned out as well as the papers report I hope we may be enabled to crush this matter and put a stop to it. I am as well as I ever was in my life. I am gaining in flesh. An active life agrees with me and I enjoy myself first rate....

I read your letters about three times and then destroy them as I do not care for any one else to read what you write to me. I want no one but myself to do that but you must take care of mine....

Yours as ever,

After the fray, deathly quiet descends on Dunker Church. Pictures like this, showing landscapes rippled in corpses, shocked a nation out of its romantic notions of war.

The summer of 1862 had begun with Union forces poised to take the Confederate capital of Richmond. By summer's end, the Federals had been chased from Richmond, and the South's commander of the Army of Northern Virginia, Robert E. Lee, had moved the war onto Union soil. By invading Maryland, he hoped its Southern sympathizers might join his depleted ranks. And he believed a decisive victory would convince Great Britain and France

Raging battle engulfs Antietam's little Dunker Church. In one Federal charge near the church, 2,300 Union men fell in just 20 minutes.

to push for Southern sovereignty.

The Confederates, numbering some 40,000, began crossing the Potomac into Maryland on September 4. Planning to divide his army and encircle the Federal garrison at Harper's Ferry, Lee issued Special Orders 191 outlining his strategy. But a copy of the secret orders found its way to General McClellan. "I have the plans of the rebels," he wrote victoriously to Lincoln, "and will catch them in their own trap."

McClellan set about clearing mountain gaps and roads leading to Harper's Ferry to ensure that Lee's army remained divided. But the Confederate forces managed to reunite near the village of Sharpsburg. In his usual deliberate way, McClellan hesitated, expecting the Rebels to withdraw across the Potomac to Virginia. They did not, and, at dawn on September 17, the Battle of Antietam, named for a creek in the area, began.

AUTUMN 1862

❖ **September 15** Stonewall Jackson captures some 12,000 Union troops at Harper's Ferry, Virginia.

❖ **September** Confederates under Kirby Smith and Braxton Bragg advance through Kentucky, taking Lexington and moving toward Louisville.

Camp Grover
September 23, 1862

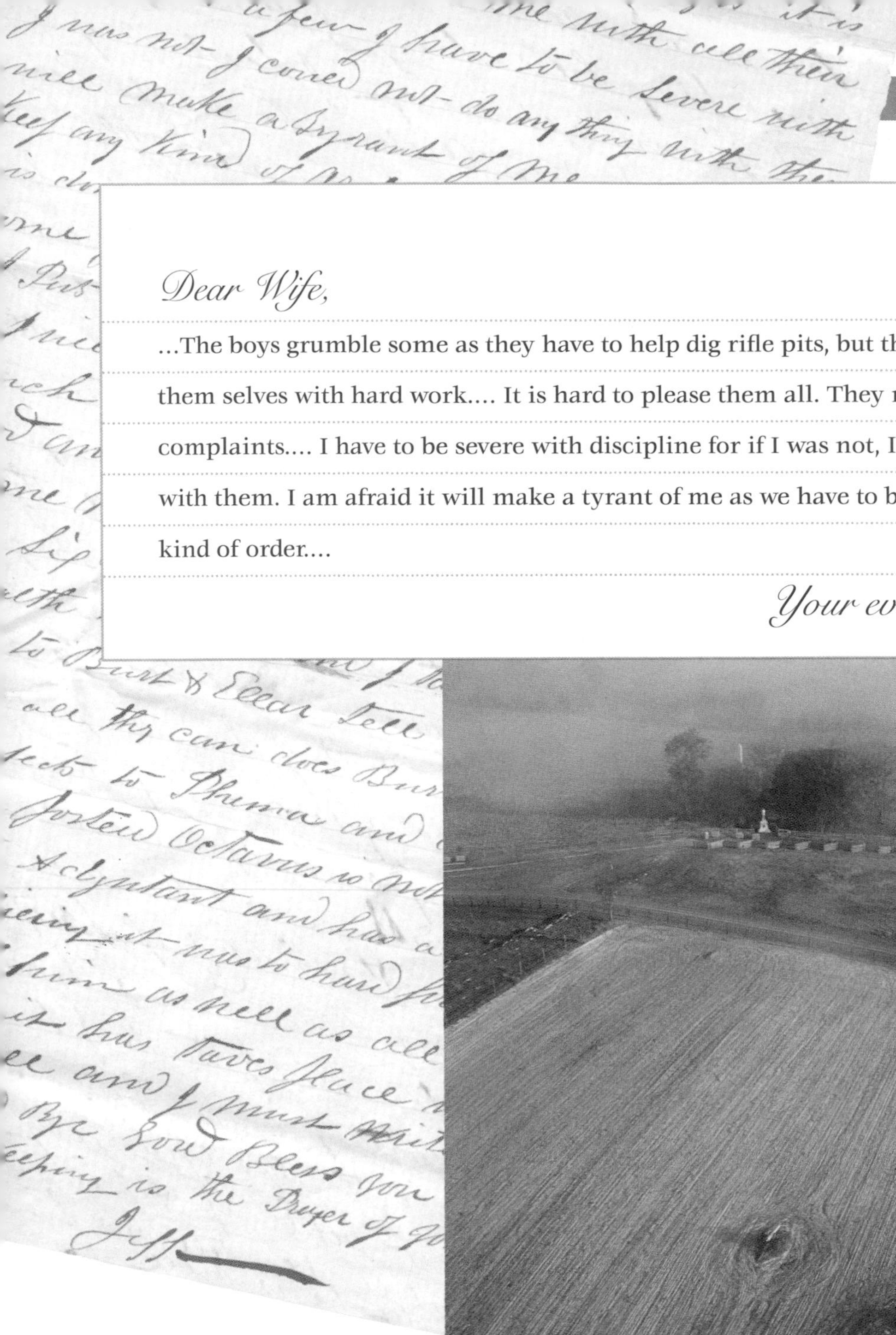

Dear Wife,

...The boys grumble some as they have to help dig rifle pits, but they do not hurt them selves with hard work.... It is hard to please them all. They run to me with... complaints.... I have to be severe with discipline for if I was not, I could not do anything with them. I am afraid it will make a tyrant of me as we have to be severe to keep any kind of order....

Your ever loving husband,

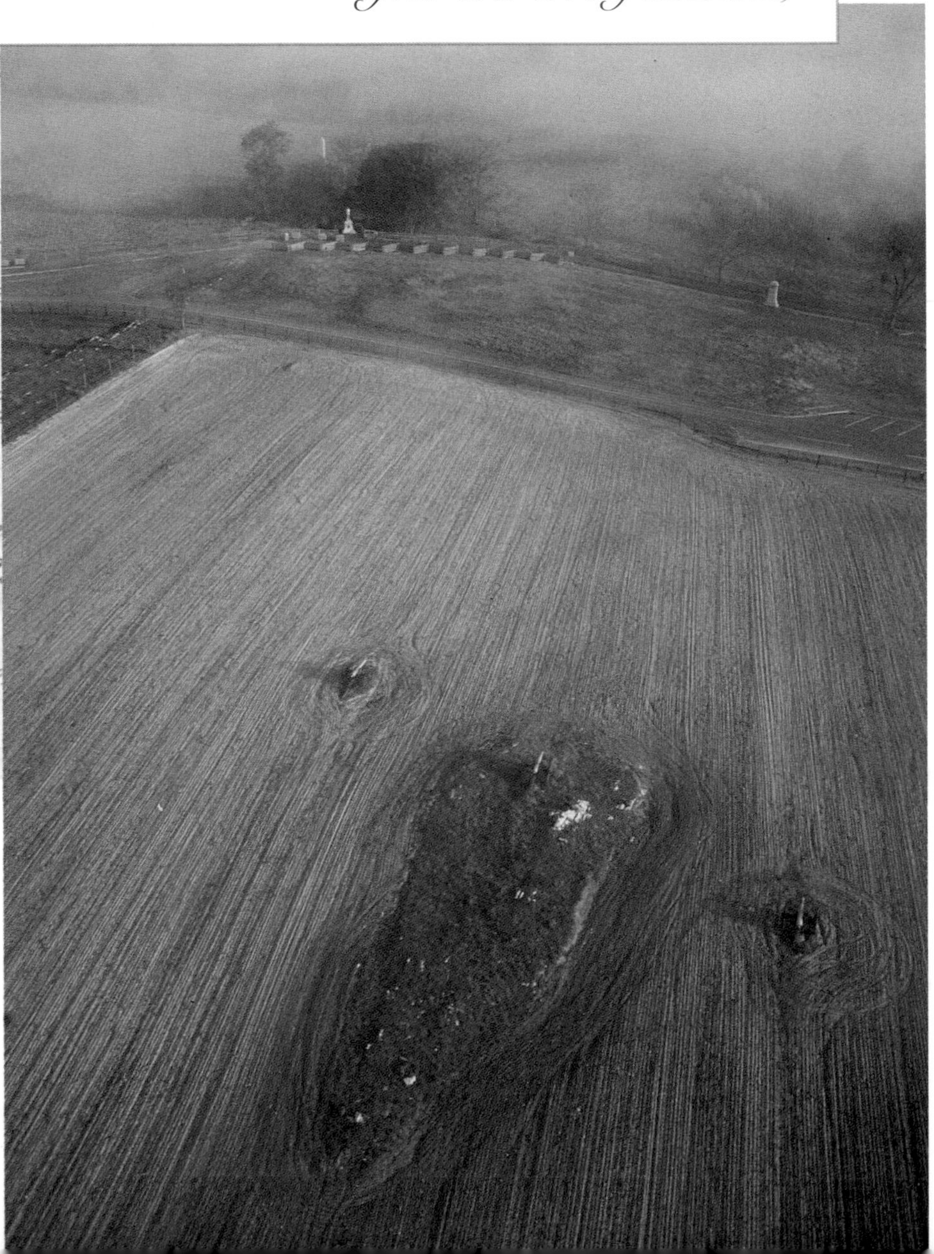

Now enshrined as a national battlefield, the serene fields of Antietam are dotted with reminders of war: Regimental monuments, cannon, and natural features recall the bloodiest one-day battle of the war. Once a simple farm road, the notorious Bloody Lane (in the background) welcomes pilgrims who come to pay homage to history.

Battle of Antietam
September 17, 1862 ✤ Late Afternoon

I CORPS
MEADE

XII CORPS
WILLIAMS

Keedysville

POTOMAC

C & O CANAL

HAGERSTOWN TURNPIKE

The Cornfield

VI CORPS
FRANKLIN

JACKSON

Dunker Church

UPPER BRIDGE

McCLELLAN
ARMY OF THE POTOMAC

McClellan's Headquarters

II CORPS
SUMNER

SUNKEN ROAD
(BLOODY LANE)

V CORPS
PORTER

LEE
ARMY OF NORTHERN VIRGINIA

LONGSTREET

MIDDLE BRIDGE

Antietam Creek

N

Lee's Headquarters

Sharpsburg

IX CORPS
BURNSIDE

LOWER BRIDGE
(BURNSIDE BRIDGE)

A. P. HILL'S DIVISION

	Union	Confederate
Infantry		
Cavalry		
Artillery		
Army hdqrs.		
Route of march		
Attack		
Retreat		

0   1 mile

0   1 kilometer

Antietam would become the bloodiest one-day battle ever fought in American history. Features of its quiet countryside would become legendary killing fields: the Cornfield, where Maj. Gen. Joseph Hooker faced off against Stonewall Jackson, and the bullets flew so thick that "every stalk of corn…was cut as closely as could have been done with a knife"; the West Woods, where Confederates inflicted 2,300 Union casualties in just 20 minutes; Bloody Lane, where Rebel soldiers repulsed waves of Yankees. Though the South enjoyed an early advantage, by midday the tide was turning and Gen. Ambrose Burnside's bluecoats were closing in on Sharpsburg. Lee knew his army had only one route of escape, a ford across the Potomac. If that was lost, so was the army.

As if by miracle, the Southern forces of Gen. A. P. Hill suddenly arrived from Harper's Ferry and launched a counterattack against Burnside. By nightfall no clear victor had emerged, but the countryside was strewn with more than 22,000 corpses—some 12,000 Union men and 10,000 Confederates. In the next days, as Lee retreated, Lincoln declared Antietam a Northern success. The South had suffered losses from which it would not recover. Even so, Union forces had not smashed Lee's army. Never again would they have such an opportunity to defeat Lee in the open field.

AUTUMN 1862

✤ **September 18** Lee retreats back into Virginia from Antietam, ending his first offensive into the North.

✤ **September 22** Lincoln issues his preliminary Emancipation Proclamation, arousing controversy among Federal troops and the Northern populace.

On Bloody Lane, fallen Southern soldiers lie behind the fence rail they used as barricade, improvising trenches in the old wagon road ruts.

CAMP GROVER
SEPTEMBER 28, 1862

Dear Wife,

...I am comfortably situated, but is no place for you here. The men are to rough, and you would be glad to get away. If we go into Winter Quarters about here and if I cannot get a furlough to go home, I will try and have you come and see me. It would be a great pleasure to have a good chat with you once again. I hope we may be permitted to see each other the comeing winter, but we must not anticipate to much....

You must not worry about me as there is no immediate danger of any battle here where we are now as it is all fortified about us. We came near being in that Battle at Antetim but moved away from there in time to get out of it. You must write often. I am so pleased to see a letter....

Your fond and loving husband,

Dr. A. A. Moulton of the 3rd New Hampshire enjoys his wife's company while encamped at Hilton Head, South Carolina. Like Halsey, many officers discouraged such visits, not wanting their spouses exposed to the "roughness" of army life.

Though men on both sides of the war lamented a lack of female companionship, women did put in appearances on the battlefield—in several different guises. Wives of officers occasionally visited their husbands in the field, sometimes with the entire family in tow. A few women even donned uniforms and served beside their spouses, either overtly or surreptitiously. Not just wives got into the fray, however. Some 400 women drawn to the soldiering life bobbed their hair, disguised their female virtues, and enlisted. Nineteen-year-old "Albert Cashier" (a.k.a. Jennie Hodgers) served three full years. Her Illinois comrades-in-arms apparently never suspected her sex, remembering

"Albert" as an acceptable, though very quiet, soldier. A Union sergeant under Gen. William S. Rosecrans did not fare so well. "He" gave birth while serving in the field, "in violation of all military law and of the army regulations."

Taking no pains to disguise their sex, legions of ladies of the night also followed the armies, setting up in nearby towns or even selling their wares out of tents along the periphery of encampments. While the Victorian mores of the time were offended by the demimondes, General Hooker maintained such a beneficent attitude toward them that, according to legend, they became known as "hookers."

AUTUMN 1862

❖ **September** In the West, Bragg halts his drive on Louisville and deploys his graycoats around Bardstown, Kentucky, calling in reinforcements.

❖ **Late September** Gen. Don Carlos Buell's bluecoats reach Louisville and continue moving toward Bragg's army.

Dear Wife,

...I went all through the Capitol Building yesterday. It is a magnifficent structure. The pictures are beautiful. The Senate Chamber is full of sick & wounded soldiers. It looked good to see ladies comeing in with delicacies for the Boys and waiting on them. I almost wished myself sick so as to get sight of and talk to a Union woman again, as we have no chance and see but few of the softer sex down here....

Your loving husband,

Founder of the American Red Cross, Clara Barton began by tending to the wounded in Washington. She then took her skills onto the battlefield.

Walt Whitman, also, served as a nurse in Washington. Devoted to Lincoln and the Union, Whitman extolled both in his poetry. Lincoln found the poet's early verses compelling for "their virility" and "unconventional sentiments."

Twin spires of Trinity Episcopal Church rise in welcome to the wounded. Like so many Washington churches, this one served as a Union hospital. So, too, did the nation's Capitol, with its half-finished new dome. In the midst of war, Lincoln insisted the construction continue, as "a sign we intend the Union shall go on."

Early in the war, incoming wounded from the Virginia battlefields turned the nation's capital into a vast hospital colony. Barracks, schools, churches, homes, public buildings—even the Capitol—were converted into makeshift wards, their rooms and hallways filled with the injured or ill.

Even though these erstwhile hospitals were abysmal by modern standards, to men who had lain

ROTUNDA DURING CIVIL WAR · 1862

The cavernous Capitol Rotunda filled with row after row of the wounded—despite the scaffolding supporting its new dome. In Washington as elsewhere, many women took on the tasks of nursing fallen soldiers.

wounded and unattended on the battlefields, they were bastions of succor. While few trained personnel were available to provide care, local women came, bringing food and a willingness to nurture. The novel concept of female nurses suddenly arose, to the displeasure of conservative doctors used to only male nurses. A strong-willed matron from Massachusetts, Dorothea L. Dix, was appointed superintendent of

women nurses and waged her own tireless battle to improve hospital conditions. Another Massachusetts native, Clara Barton, began caring for the wounded at the outset of the war. In April 1861 the shy Patent Office clerk overcame her timidity to aid a Massachusetts regiment whose men had been mobbed on their way to Washington. By 1862 she had taken her nursing abilities onto the battlefield.

Probably the most eloquent of Washington's nurses was poet Walt Whitman, who saw in the city's aspect "America, already brought to Hospital in her fair youth, in this great whited sepulchre of Washington itself."

CAMP NEAR FORT ELLSWORTH
OCTOBER 4, 1862

My Dear Wife,

...I am glad to hear of the continued good health of you and the Little Ones we love. My own health is good as is also the Company, excepting the measels. I had them when a child. I can remember it as I was very sick.... Do you miss the young men out of Dover? I should think the girls would be lonesome....

I have just looked at my watch and find it is 1/4 past three, the children off to Sundy school and you are at home—it may be reading the Bible and once in a while wondering where Jeff is and what he is doing.... I make out to enjoy myself as I am not the one to worry. I have many a good hearty laugh as laughing does one good and a long face is something that I seldom wear....

I am thankfull to...Burt and my little girl for the candy. I have got the last in my mouth now....

Your loveing husband,

"Young Napoleon" George McClellan (top) was called. But he didn't fight like Napoleon and was replaced by Ambrose Burnside (right), whose whiskers inspired the term "sideburns."

"McClellan is to me one of the mysteries of the war," Grant once said. Grant was not alone. McClellan seemed to defy definition. Vainglorious and opinionated, he was also a talented organizer, creating and taking command of the Army of the Potomac at the age of 34 and soon, through his own machinations, becoming commander of all Union armies.

But in the field he perpetually hesitated. In both the Peninsula Campaign and at Antietam he overestimated enemy strength and lost superb opportunities to crush Lee's army. When McClellan delayed in pursuing Lee after Antietam, Lincoln's patience was exhausted, and he appointed Ambrose Burnside as the new commander of the Army of the Potomac, a compromise choice. Constantly plagued by a lack of strong generals, Lincoln would pit several different commanders against Lee in the course of the war.

"Few men, probably, have risen so high upon so slight a foundation...," a Massachusetts colonel said of Burnside. Even Burnside doubted his fitness for the position and refused it twice before finally accepting. Apparently, he accepted out of fear that, if he refused, the command would be offered to his nemesis, General Hooker. Ironically, Burnside's fears—on all counts— would soon be realized.

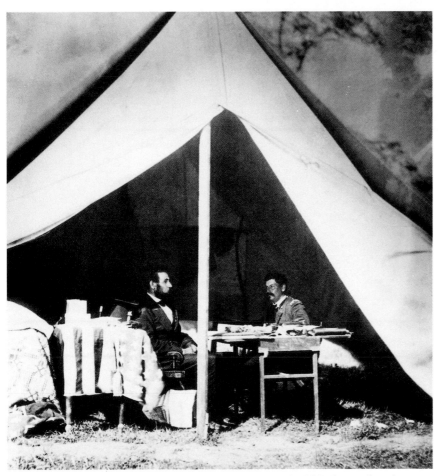

Lincoln visits McClellan in the field in the autumn of 1862. Soon after, he relieved McClellan as commander of the Army of the Potomac.

Photographer Mathew B. Brady, wearing his characteristic straw hat, shares a quiet moment with General Burnside.

AUTUMN 1862

❖ **October 4** Gen. William Rosecrans defeats Rebel forces under Gen. Earl Van Dorn at the Battle of Corinth in Mississippi.

❖ **October 8** After the inconclusive Battle of Perryville, Bragg and Smith abandon the Southern campaign to take Kentucky and retreat into Tennessee.

Though Antietam had ended in no conclusive victory, it had halted Lee's advance into the North. Lincoln hailed it as a victory—one he had been impatiently awaiting. Since July, the President had been anxious for a military success to sweeten the public mood before making a critical—and controversial—announcement. Now he had it, and on September 22, 1862, he issued the preliminary Emancipation Proclamation. Effective as of January 1, slaves of all those who supported rebellion would be free.

His proclamation turned war politics in a new direction and alienated much of the Democratic Party, the Northern public, and his own officers, among them the outspoken George McClellan. The North had gone to war to restore the Union, not abolish slavery. In fact, in February 1861, Congress had passed a 13th Amendment, guaranteeing

that the Federal government would not interfere with a state's internal slavery policies. But war overtook the country before the amendment could be sent to the states for ratification, and after a year and a half of fighting, anti-Southern—and with it pro-abolitionist—sentiment had mounted in the capital.

In July, Congress had passed a confiscation act, decreeing that the government could confiscate the property of "traitors," including slaves; escaped slaves were "deemed captives of war" and "forever free." Throughout the South, blacks flocked to Federal contraband camps, where, while not necessarily treated well, they were nonetheless given the first taste of freedom they had ever experienced.

The issue of freeing the South's slaves was a practical one at that point. "The slaves were undeniably an element of strength to those who

had their service," Lincoln said, "and we must decide whether that element should be with us or against us." Still, Lincoln hesitated over emancipation policy, knowing how controversial it would be and fearing it might alienate the border states of Maryland, Kentucky, and Missouri. Should they side with the South, valuable resources and manpower would fall into the hands of the enemy. The President had even proposed a "compensated emancipation" to the border states, offering to pay for the freeing of their slaves. They were not interested.

In an open letter to his critic, columnist Horace Greeley, Lincoln said flatly: "If I could save the Union without freeing *any* slave I would do it, and if I could save it by freeing *all* the slaves I would do it." In the end, he chose freedom, and, as unpopular as his move was in his own nation, it garnered tremendous

support in Europe. Britain, who had harbored sympathy for the Confederate states' rights to self-determination, now saw the war as a battle for human rights, with the North championing a moral cause. France, then under Napoleon III, followed Britain's lead. "The Emancipation Proclamation has done more for us," Henry Adams wrote from Europe, "than all our former victories and all our diplomacy."

Lincoln also had good news from the West that autumn. A Rebel offensive aimed at the strategic railroad junction of Corinth, Mississippi, had been foiled. And a month-long invasion of Kentucky by Gen. Braxton Bragg had finally ended with the Battle of Perryville. Lincoln had been adamant that his home state not join the Confederacy, saying that, while he hoped to have God on his side, he must have Kentucky.

U.S. After Start of Civil War ❖ Late 1861

Free state
Slave state
Territory

0   600 miles
0   900 kilometers

On the road to freedom, slaves (opposite) follow bluecoats. In 1861 Union Gen. Benjamin Butler declared escaped slaves "contraband of war," safe from their owners. His policy brought hope—and problems.

Sunlight streaks the battle-scarred ground of Perryville, Kentucky. Though the fighting here in October 1862 produced no true victor, it did end the Confederate attempt to claim that rich border state.

Dear Wife,

...I am willing to do all that is in my power for the men and their families. The men are all satisfied, I think. I treat them well and am doing all I can to make them comfortable... We had one death in camp yesterdy. A...man from Sussex. We buried him last night by moon light. It was very solemn. The band played a Funeral March and there was three volies fired over his grave....

Your ever loveing husband,

Trumpeting patriotism and the excitement of battle, recruitment posters urge men to enlist. Many recruits signed on with companies composed of friends and neighbors. But esprit de corps, patriotism, and the glamour of war were not enough to fill the ranks. State recruitment offices in the North offered cash bounties to men willing to join up. Still, it was the early "veteran volunteers" like Halsey who proved the best fighters.

Enticing men into the army was far easier in the first blush of war, when the romance of battle outweighed its realities. In 1861 both sides were inundated with volunteers, but the surfeit lasted only briefly. Soon "war meetings" were being held across the divided nation, with choirs, orators, and elderly veterans on hand to inspire new volunteers. "It needed only the first man to step forward...be patted on the back...and cheered...as the hero of the hour, when a second, a third, and a fourth would follow."

Sometimes a man who had served previously in the army or militia would circulate an enlistment sheet among his friends and neighbors. Then, proceeding to a recruitment office, the group of signatories would enlist together and form a company, with the man who had initially circulated the petition commissioned as its captain.

Sent first to training camps, new recruits sometimes naively brought their wives and children along. Since many of the camps were ineffectual, regiments set off to war woefully undertrained. One historian reported that these raw soldiers, when "trying to execute the order to charge bayonet stuck one another." Still, the war pitched on and the recruiting process followed. In the last two years of the conflict, more than a million new volunteers joined the Union cause.

AUTUMN 1862

❖ **October 9-12** Confederate cavalry commander J. E. B. (Jeb) Stuart and a force of 1,800 men make a second historic ride around McClellan's army—126 miles through Maryland and Pennsylvania. In a raid on the Pennsylvania town of Chambersburg, Stuart's forces capture some 500 Federal horses.

ALEXANDRIA, VA. OCTOBER 18, 1862
SATURDAY NIGHT ¼ PAST SIX

My Dear Wife,

...I am glad that you make yourself so useful in looking after our affairs. It will do you no harm, I suppose. It seems somewhat strange...as I always looked after everything....

I mean to go to church here in Alexandria...then I will write you, and you must excuse me if I look and see what kind of ladies they have down here in Secession. You wish to know what kind of a place this is. Well, it is pleasantly situated on the Potomac River, which is a mile wide here. It is a city of 12000 inhabitants.... There are a good many fine places in the town and a good many rickety old concerns where the Blacks and poor white trash live. There are a great many Secessionists here, and they of course do not like us Northern Yankees but have to keep quiet. There are eleven large Hospitals in the place and there are thousands of sick and wounded men. Almost all of the churches are Hospitals....

Everything is war. It is an offensive affair this fighting and I hope it will not last much longer for it must ruin this or any other country to keep such an immense army in the field.... Our Boys are well contented. They do not appear to get home sick. Their duties are light where we now are and they feel anxious to stay here. They can fish, and oysters are cheap if they have the money to buy them, but money is a scarce commodity in our Regt.... I hope all the families of my men get their State pay....

Your affectionate and loveing husband,

Union soldiers lounge at Arlington House, once the Lees' gracious northern Virginia home.

Lee's boyhood home in Alexandria was the property of his mother's relatives.

A Virginia sutler takes advantage of the Union appetite for oysters.

Ironically, the Union troops encamped throughout northern Virginia were occupying Robert E. Lee's home soil. Lee grew up in a town house in Alexandria, Virginia, in conditions of genteel poverty. His roots went deep into the old Virginia aristocracy. His father was Revolutionary War hero Gen. Henry "Lighthorse Harry" Lee and his mother, Ann Carter, was descended from a distinguished and socially prominent Virginia family. After graduating second in his class at West Point, Lee married a distant cousin, Mary Custis, the daughter of George Washington's adopted son.

Though the couple spent most of their early life moving from one army post to the next, they considered their permanent home to be the Greek revival mansion of Mary's childhood—Arlington House. Commanding a hillside on the Potomac River overlooking Washington, Arlington House was commandeered by the Union in 1861. In 1864, in a vindictive move against the Confederate hero, the Union quartermaster general made the mansion grounds a Federal cemetery—the beginnings of Arlington National Cemetery.

After the war the Lees never returned to their home, but Robert once wrote that at Arlington House his "affections and attachments" were "more strongly placed than at any other place in the world."

Unaware of the fate awaiting them, Lee and his second eldest son, "Rooney," appear hopeful and contented in the 1840s, when Lee was a rising star in the U.S. Army. Later, Lee and the Harvard-educated Rooney would fight against that very army. A "scientific fighter," the younger Lee distinguished himself as an officer in Jeb Stuart's cavalry and was held captive for nine months in a Union prison.

ALEXANDRIA
OCTOBER 26, 1862

Dear Wife,

...I had quite a time with Ed Kinny to day. He got drunk this morning and got on one of his tantrums. I tried to quiet him but could not. He struck at me, and I had to tye him and he went on at a terrible rate.... I shall have to have him tried by a Court Martial. Rum causes me a good deal of trouble, and I fear it will, as we are here in the City where the men can get it. I mean to break up all the Rum Shops I can find after this. I wish there were none in the county....

I hope you are not going to be much sick. You must not work to hard cleaning house. You did not tell me what ailed you. I ment you to tell me every thing. I do you. I am as hearty and fat as a Pig. Get fat every day. My appetite is fine. I do not drink much tea or coffee. Eat mostly sweet potatoes, bread & butter & fresh meat. Had mush for supper and will have mush fried for breakfast. We have an excellent cook. He can cook tomatoes firstrate. He is a very quiet fellow....

Your own loveing husband,

Renowned wartime photographer Mathew B. Brady sports his trademark attire in this shot. "A spirit in my feet said 'Go,'" the flamboyant Brady explained, "and I went."

Lashed spread-eagle to a wagon wheel, a soldier suffers the standard punishment for drunkenness. The drink itself could be punishment enough, described by one soldier as a blend of "bark juice, tarwater, turpentine, brown sugar, lamp-oil and alcohol."

Brady's box camera, made in New York City, dates from 1860. The type of lens suggests the camera was used for portraits.

Soldiers solemnly pose for posterity. So popular did such wartime portraits become that writer Oliver Wendell Holmes called them "the social currency, the sentimental greenbacks of civilization." Below, a "whatisit" wagon—actually a mobile darkroom—trudges after the army.

In the 1860s photography was a fledgling art, begun some 20 years earlier by French painter Louis Jacques Mandé Daguerre. When the Civil War broke out, American practitioners of this new craft realized its potential for recording history and flocked to the battlefields. Some photographers served as official government documenters, many others were independents—and some were spies.

Burdened by their cumbersome equipment, these early photographers loaded their strange, tented "whatisit" wagons with fragile glass plates, chemicals, bulky cameras, and camera stands, and followed the armies over rough terrain. Unable as yet to capture action shots, they left that to the illustrators and contented themselves with before-and-after the battle stills or portraits of men proudly posed in uniform.

Most famous among the wartime photographers was Mathew B. Brady. Brady was born in New York State and by the war's advent had established himself as the preferred photographer of the country's elite. His legendary collection of 7,500 war photographs, taken as often by his assistants as by Brady himself, now resides in the Library of Congress. Ironically, the thousands of images he and his staff made cost Brady an estimated $100,000 and ran him to financial ruin. He died poor and in obscurity in 1896.

AUTUMN 1862

❖ **October 30** Buell is replaced by General Rosecrans as commander of the Union Army of the Cumberland.

❖ **November** From the Tennessee border Grant launches his months-long campaign to take the Confederate port of Vicksburg, Mississippi.

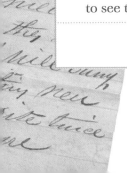

ALEXANDRIA, VA.
OCTOBER 29, 1862

Dear Wife,

...You need not send me any apples, as I can by them here what I need. Keep them for your own use. I want you should have a good liveing. I think we shall be paid off next week or the week after and then I can send you money....

I have a good deal more power than when I first took charge here. All I have to do is to sit in my office and give orders and over see the soldiers.... I think the bosses must like me or they would not give me so good a job. The whole of the regiment begrudge me my job as the duty they are doing is not very pleasant....

You may continue to take the Jerseyman and send it to me as I can afford it and want to see the county news....

Good night,

AS OF OCTOBER 1862:

ARMY OF THE POTOMAC
COMMANDED BY MAJ. GEN. GEORGE B. MCCLELLAN

THIRD CORPS
COMMANDED BY MAJ. GEN. GEORGE STONEMAN

SECOND DIVISION
COMMANDED BY BRIG. GEN. DANIEL E. SICKLES

FIRST BRIGADE (CARR'S BRIGADE)
COMMANDED BY BRIG. GEN. JOSEPH B. CARR

11TH REGIMENT (NEW JERSEY VOLUNTEERS)
COMMANDED BY COL. ROBERT MCALLISTER

COMPANY E
COMMANDED BY CAPT. THOMAS J. HALSEY

Robert McAllister

Stephen Moore

John Schoonover

Edward L. Welling

AS OF AUGUST 1862:

11TH NEW JERSEY VOLUNTEERS

FIELD AND STAFF OFFICERS:

COL. ROBERT MCALLISTER
LT. COL. STEPHEN MOORE
MAJ. VALENTINE MUTCHLER
ADJUTANT JOHN SCHOONOVER
QUARTERMASTER GARRET SCHENCK
EDWARD L. WELLING, SURGEON
EDWARD BYINGTON, ASST. SURGEON
EDWIN B. YOUNG, ASST. SURGEON
FREDERICK KNIGHTON, CHAPLAIN

NON-COMMISSIONED STAFF:

SGT. MAJOR WILLIAM J. MOUNT
QUARTERMASTER SGT. GEORGE C. BOICE
COMMISSARY SGT. PHILIP D. CRISP
GEORGE T. RIBBLE, HOSPITAL STEWARD
GEORGE F. DURANT, DRUM MAJOR

COMPANY E

CAPT. THOMAS J. HALSEY
1ST LT. EDWARD E. S.
   NEWBERRY
2ND LT. SILAS W. VOLK
7 SERGEANTS
6 CORPORALS
83 PRIVATES
1 MUSICIAN
1 WAGONER

THE ORIGINAL 979 MEN OF
THE 11TH REGIMENT WERE
MUSTERED IN ON AUGUST
18, 1862 AT CAMP PERRINE,
TRENTON, NEW JERSEY.

The infantry followed an organization that began at the company level, proceeded through regiments, brigades, divisions, corps, and armies. Since many high-ranking officers of the North and the South had been trained at West Point, the structure of their armies followed a similar design. There were, however, important differences. The Union named its armies after major bodies of water in their regions of operation—for example, the Army of the Potomac. The South named its armies after larger areas of operation—for example, the Army of Northern Virginia.

More important than differences in naming were the differences in approach toward sustaining regiments. As Union regiments lost men, they were not necessarily replaced with new recruits. When a regiment fell to 150 to 200 men, it was often disbanded and new regiments were formed from the remnants of the old. This cost the North a sense of esprit de corps that bolstered the Southern army, which kept regiments intact by adding new recruits. Halsey's regiment was rare in that it remained intact from the beginning of the war to the end.

Confederate soldiers also elected all officers below the rank of brigadier general. As one historian explained it, "They were electing men whom they were willing to trust with their lives, so you better believe they selected the best men."

Photographs at left depict members of Halsey's regiment. Of the 979 men mustered in at the onset of the war, 249 were killed and 360 were wounded. The chart (top) illustrates where the 11th fit in the hierarchy of the Army of the Potomac. Normally, a regiment contained 10-12 companies; a brigade, 2 or more regiments; a division, 2 or more brigades; and a corps, 2 or more divisions.

George T. Ribble

Silas W. Volk

William J. Mount

Edward E. S. Newberry

Dear Wife,

...Ed Kinny has had his trial but I do not know what his sentence will be. I am in hopes it will be a lesson to the rest to keep sober....

I see by the papers today that McCllelan has been relieved of the command of the Army.... We are here to put this war through and mean to do it. Remember me to...the children and all enquiring friends. I remain as ever,

Your affectionate husband

P.S. I saw the Monitor yesterday. She passed down by here, and I had a fair view of her.

"Modern" monster, the 275-foot C.S.S. *Virginia* claims her first victim, the 24-gun warship U.S.S. *Cumberland.* In her initial foray, the South's invincible ironclad sank one other enemy warship and ran off three more.

The South had gone to war with virtually no sea power and no means to create it. Reasoning that "inequality of numbers may be compensated for by invulnerability," the secretary of the non-existent Confederate Navy ordered his engineers to design a single unsinkable warship.

Resurrecting the U.S.S. *Merrimack*, a Federal steam frigate that Union troops had scuttled, engineers transformed her into what they called "an ironclad" and renamed her the C.S.S. *Virginia*. Learning of this awesome new weapon, the North hurried to design a response.

On March 8, 1862, the *Virginia* steamed into Hampton Roads, at the end of the Virginia Peninsula. The projectiles hurled at her bounced off like "peas from a popgun," and she made quick work of the enemy. But her rule of the waves was short-lived. By nightfall the North's new ironclad, the U.S.S. *Monitor,* had come to the rescue.

In the morning the two ships squared off in a four-hour battle that ended in a draw. Lincoln, fearing the loss of the *Monitor,* ordered that she "be not too much exposed." So for two months the unchallenged *Virginia* harassed Union ships in Hampton Roads. In early May she was finally defanged when Federal troops captured her base, Norfolk. With no escape route available to her, the Confederates blew her up.

Battle of the Ironclads off Fort Monroe, Virginia, ended in a draw but changed the course of naval warfare. To spectators, the South's *Virginia* looked like a floating roof and the North's *Monitor* like "a cheese box on a raft." At left, *Monitor* crew members relax on deck.

AUTUMN 1862

❖ **November 4** Republicans lose ground in congressional and state elections in the North.

❖ **November 7** Ambrose Burnside replaces McClellan as commander of the Army of the Potomac and makes plans to march on Fredericksburg, Virginia.

ALEXANDRIA, VA.
NOVEMBER 12, 1862

Dear Wife,

...I see that you are selling the corn. I am glad that you can sell it as it helps you to get

along. It looks dull about getting our pay and if you had no way to get money, I do not

know what you would do, but there is always some way to get along, I think....

There has been some talk about our going on to the Front but I hardly think we will

go as there are so many sick that the Regiment is small....

If you have not got your tax bill, you can ask Mr. Ball to go to Munson Store and get

it. I would like to know how much my taxes are both on the farm and house....

NOVEMBER 13

It is warm like spring this morning. I have my coat off and the windows are up. I sup-

pose the snow will soon go up home, and you will have Indian summer yet.

Yours as ever,

Pay, when it came at last, briefly broke the tedium of life in the field. Men might stake some of their newfound cash on a game of cards or visit the sutler's row (below) in the closest town. Halsey and other men had much of their pay sent directly to their families via allotment checks.

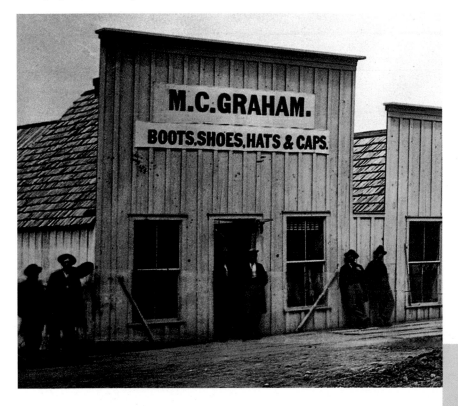

All kinds of currency circulated during the war, from Confederate bills worth very little to Northern banknotes issued by individual banks (opposite). Faced with a worsening financial crisis early in 1862, the United States printed its own paper money—"greenbacks"—legal tender unbacked by gold or silver. As one senator from Vermont prophesied, "the doors of the temple of paper money would not soon again be closed."

One of the thorniest problems faced by Civil War soldiers was that of pay. While both Federal and Confederate regulations called for payment to be made every other month, that rarely happened, and the soldier, as well as his family, suffered in consequence. For officers like Halsey, who had to buy their own food, the situation could be particularly grim. One officer recalled a day when he had only a slice of watermelon to eat.

Northern men sometimes went six months without pay, and Southerners as long as a year. Such irregularity only encouraged desertion and poor morale. In the Union Army, the paymaster general typically withheld salaries until men were about to depart for battle. Then his minions would appear, producing "more joy in camp than is said to have been produced in heaven over the one sinner that repenteth." While merrymaking and easy spending followed, many men were more concerned with their pay reaching the home front. By signing allotment rolls, they could send a portion of their salaries directly to their families.

While a captain, Halsey would have received $115.50 a month, plus an additional sum for serving as adjutant. A private received only $13, but with unemployment high, some men were probably enticed by this "regular" salary. However, while the army itself may have been "regular," its payments, sadly, were not.

AUTUMN 1862

❖ **November 17** The 115,000-man Army of the Potomac reaches the north bank of the Rappahannock, across from Fredericksburg. While the bluecoats await pontoon bridges to cross the river, Lee's army moves into the city, taking up defensive positions on the heights.

NOVEMBER 20, 1862
ABOUT 10 MILES EAST OF FAIR FAX COURT HOUSE
IN THE WOODS AND IN THE MUD

My Dear Wife,

We are now campaigning in earnest. It is warm and it has

rained for two days and the roads are horrible and our camp

is all mud. We are waiting for our rations to come up and

then for a 40 mile march to Fredricksburgh and then on to

some other place, I presume Richmond is the point....

I slept right on the ground with my rubber blanket

under me and do not take any cold. I am well and hearty

yet and keep as hungry as a bear. I enjoy this kind of life

finely, although I presume I shall get enough of it before I

get through.... I send home some Secesh Postage Stamps and

a Rebel flag found in a rebel camp....

Your affectionate husband,

Halsey's rubber blanket probably resembled this one. Fastened by grommets, such blankets were first issued in November 1861.

From the first weeks of hostilities, the North had aimed its sights on Richmond, hoping that the fall of the Confederate capital would bring an end to the Southern rebellion. Besides its symbolic worth, the city was home to the Tredegar Iron Works, where much of the Confederacy's guns, railroad iron, and munitions was produced. Gen. Irvin McDowell, spurred on by Lincoln and a press shouting "Forward to Richmond!" had made the initial move toward the city, but that ended in the debacle at First Manassas. His successor, McClellan, then launched the massive and months-long Peninsula Campaign the following spring, only to be stopped by Lee at Richmond's door. The next winter, Burnside tried to come at the city from the north, with terrible results for himself and his army.

During the spring of 1862, McClellan marched 100,000 men and 260 cannon up the Virginia Peninsula toward Richmond.

Ironically, Richmond had not originally espoused war. Most of its population was Unionist, and the Old Dominion was not a strong slave state. But when Lincoln called Virginia volunteers to fight against the Deep South, Richmonders turned their face on the Union and became ardent—and long-suffering—Confederates. Even as the privations of war overtook the once genteel city, Richmonders refused to give up their distinctive élan. Well-heeled young socialites gallantly formed a Starvation Club, whose refreshmentless soirees found them "dancing on the edge of the grave."

AUTUMN 1862

❖ **November 30** Stonewall Jackson's forces arrive in Fredericksburg.

❖ **December 11** Union troops cross the Rappahannock to Fredericksburg.

❖ **December 11** Confederates under Nathan Bedford Forrest raid Grant's communications lines in Tennessee.

SUNDAY, DECEMBER 14, 1862
ON THE FIELD OF BATTLE

Dear Wife,

I am still alive and well, thank God. The bullets & shells have been whistling about us nearly all the time. The battle has been going on for 4 days. Yesterday was a fearful day. Many a poor fellow lost his life. I was where we could see the fight. The roar of Artillery and the crash of small arms was terriffic.... Our regiment have been out skirmishing to day. We have lost two men and had five wounded. My company has not been out yet. Our time will soon come, I suppose we shall have a big fight to morrow. The Rebels are in a strong position on the Hills in the rear of Fredricksburg and we shall have a hard time of it to dislodge them. CONTINUED...

Naturally defended by the Rappahannock River, Fredericksburg and its troublesome waterfront repeatedly challenged the Union Army. Midway between Washington and Richmond, the town and its environs saw four major battles between 1862 and 1864. Here, Federals guarding the river take advantage of a lull in the Second Battle of Fredericksburg, fought in the spring of 1863.

HARPER'S WEEKLY.

A JOURNAL OF CIVILIZATION.

VOL. VI.—No. 313.]

NEW YORK, SATURDAY, DECEMBER 27, 1862.

Entered according to Act of Congress, in the Year 1862, by Harper & Brothers, in the Clerk's Office of the District Court for the Southern District of New York.

[SINGLE COPIES SIX CENTS.
$2 50 PER YEAR IN ADVANCE.

THE ATTACK ON FREDERICKSBURG—THE FORLORN HOPE SCALING THE HILL.—[SEE PAGE 830.]

Braving Rebel sharp-shooters, Union soldiers ferry across the Rappahannock, hoping to chase the snipers off and establish a beachhead. More Union troops soon followed in their wake, crossing the river on pontoon bridges.

I hope we may be successfull in this fight. If we are not, I fear the War will not soon end, and oh, how I wish it might be closed with Honor and that our beloved Land might once more be unitted and happy as it once was. There has been no general engagement to day, I suppose in conesquince of its being Sunday. I am glad of it....

We have no tents with us and we have to sleep on the ground, officers and all and the nights are cold. We get up in the morning and find it all mud under us as the warmth from our bodies thaws the ground. It is wonderful what men can stand. I should think we would all get sick, but it seems as though we can get accustomed to almost anything....

I do not feel prepared to die. If I was, I should not care so much to go on the Field of Battle. I am trying to look to God for guidance in these trying times....

Your affectionate husband,

Patterns of war: Today rows of gravestones etch the ridgetop known as Marye's Heights. Some 27,000 Union men hurled themselves at the 6,000 Confederates holding this high ground in the winter of 1862. But to no avail. The assault across this open ground claimed 8,000 Union men.

When the reluctant Ambrose Burnside took command of the Army of the Potomac in November, he was well aware that Lincoln wanted an immediate move against Lee. He obliged with a plan to take Fredericksburg, a strategic Virginia town and railroad junction midway between Washington and Richmond. His stratagem called for moving troops first southwest toward Warrenton, in a feint to confuse Lee, then marching quickly on to poorly defended Fredericksburg. Lincoln had some doubts about the plan, telling Burnside it would succeed only "if you move very rapidly; otherwise not."

Burnside did move rapidly, but when he arrived on the banks of the Rappahannock River across from Fredericksburg, the pontoons he needed to build bridges to town were nowhere in sight. Five days later they arrived, but, with Southern sharpshooters picking off his engineers, it took another two weeks to complete the bridges.

On December 11, when Federal troops at last began crossing the Rappahannock, Lee was ready for them. He had secured Marye's Heights, a hill above the town, and his entire army, 72,500 men, was positioned in the area to meet Burnside's 106,000 men—in total, the greatest concentration of troops to face off in the war.

On December 12, as Burnside moved more divisions into Fredericksburg, Lee moved Stonewall Jackson's corps, positioned downstream, closer to the front. When the bluecoats finally attacked the following morning, Lee had a seven-mile-long front in place to greet them.

Throughout the long day of battle the Federals penetrated the Confederate lines only once along the southern flank—and then only briefly. In the town itself, thousands of Union soldiers struggled vainly uphill toward the impregnable Southern defenses deployed on Marye's Heights. Watching, Lee commented drily, "It is well that war is so terrible—we should grow too fond of it." By day's end the North had suffered 12,700 casualties, the South 5,300.

That bitter cold night the bodies of the dead and wounded littered the frozen ground, as Rebel scavengers worked the battlefield, divesting the fallen of their warm uniforms. Bereft, Burnside planned a new assault for the morning, one

that he himself would lead. His officers managed to dissuade him, but they could not ease his anguish. "Oh, those men! Oh, those men!" he grieved, "I am thinking of them all the time." A war correspondent, reporting on the slaughter, summed up the day, "It can hardly be in human nature for men to show more valor, or generals to manifest less judgement."

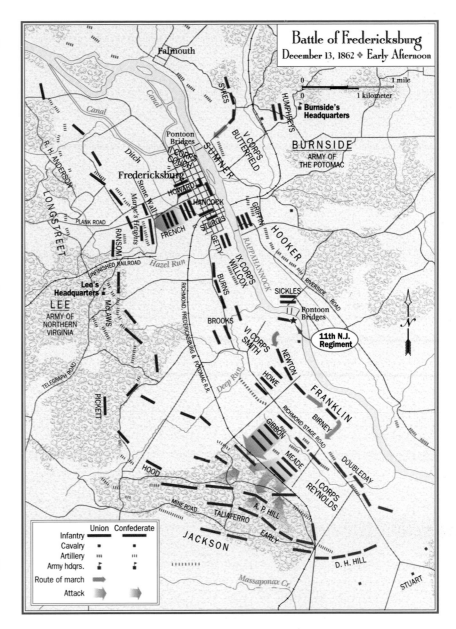

Battle of Fredericksburg
December 13, 1862 ❖ Early Afternoon

Falmouth

Burnside's Headquarters

BURNSIDE
ARMY OF THE POTOMAC

Pontoon Bridges

Fredericksburg

Stone Wall

Marye's Heights

Canal

Ditch

R. H. ANDERSON

LONGSTREET

PLANK ROAD

RANSOM

UNFINISHED RAILROAD

Lee's Headquarters

LEE
ARMY OF NORTHERN VIRGINIA

McLAWS

TELEGRAPH ROAD

PICKET

HOOD

MINE ROAD

TALIAFERRO

JACKSON

SYKES

HUMPHREYS

V CORPS BUTTERFIELD

I CORPS COUCH

SUMNER

HOWARD

HANCOCK

FRENCH

STURGIS

GETTY

IX CORPS WILLCOX

BURNS

BROOKS

GRIFFIN

HOOKER

RAPPAHANNOCK

RIVERSIDE ROAD

SICKLES

Pontoon Bridges

11th N.J. Regiment

VI CORPS SMITH

NEWTON

HOWE

FRANKLIN

BIRNEY

GIBBON

MEADE

DOUBLEDAY

I CORPS REYNOLDS

A. P. HILL

EARLY

D. H. HILL

STUART

RICHMOND, FREDERICKSBURG & POTOMAC R.R.

RICHMOND STAGE ROAD

Hazel Run

Deep Run

Massaponax Cr.

0 ___ 1 mile
0 ___ 1 kilometer

N

	Union	Confederate
Infantry	▬	▬
Cavalry	∎	∎
Artillery	⊞	⊞
Army hdqrs.	♟	♟
Route of march	➡	
Attack	➡	➡

WINTER 1862

❖ **December 15** The Union Army retreats across the Rappahannock.

❖ **December 20** Grant's Vicksburg advance is thwarted when Rebel forces destroy his Holly Springs supply base.

❖ **December 20** William Tecumseh Sherman heads toward Vicksburg.

IN CAMP NEAR FREDRICKSBURG
DECEMBER 22, 1862

My Dear Wife,

...I have only fifty men fit for duty and half of them have bad colds. The Picket lines can be traced on both sides by the mens coughing. Poor fellows. How I pity them and the sick. It is trying on them. No kind hands to minister to their wants and far to many of the Doctors are unfit for the place they fill. They come for money. I fear such is the hard truth. The men say if you have the Diarhea, they give you three Pills, and if you are costive, they give you the same dose, and the same for nearly every thing....

I hear that you are expecting me home, that I have resigned. It is news to me. I could not resign if I wanted to. Not as long as I am well. There are a good many Officers resigning as they cannot stand a Winter Campaign....

Your loveing husband,

George T. Ribble served as assistant surgeon in the 11th New Jersey Volunteers.

Tools of the trade in a Confederate surgeon's instrument kit reflect the primary goal of surgery— amputation. Little else could be done for patients with severe tissue wounds or bone injuries.

"The Civil War was fought at the end of the medical Middle Ages," a surgeon general said after the war. With the study of bacteriology in its infancy, infection and lack of sanitation were not yet linked. Doctors flicked surgical knives on their boots to clean them and probed wounds with hands that, at most, had been washed in cold water. Drunk and incompetent surgeons were not unheard of, and "contract doctors," hired early in the war, were often charlatans or out of practice. Among the enlisted physicians, many were country doctors ill-suited to treat men in the field. Yet, by 19th-century standards, Civil War doctors saved more patients of dis-

ease than doctors working in the Mexican or Spanish-American Wars.

By war's end, 15,000 surgeons had served in both armies. A Federal ambulance corps had been established and a sanitation commission formed. Its tireless general secretary, landscape architect Frederick Law Olmsted, helped organize volunteers to distribute food, clothing, and medical supplies to men in the field.

Though the South's medical corps also became better organized as the war went on, it suffered from lack of supplies, drugs, and rail lines to ship men and equipment to hospitals. "Our poor sick, I know, suffer much...," Lee said.

The waiting wounded: At a Federal collection point near Richmond the injured receive treatment and await evacuation to a hospital. In the course of battle, the fallen were treated at divisional field hospitals and later taken, if necessary, to better-equipped general hospitals.

WINTER 1862-1863

❖ **December 31** U.S.S. *Monitor* sinks in a storm off North Carolina.

❖ **January 1** Lincoln issues a finalized Emancipation Proclamation.

❖ **January 2** Battle of Stone's River ends. Bragg loses a third of his army to Rosecrans's Federals, outside Murfreesborough, Tennessee.

The year 1862 ended in frustration for the Union. Lee's Army of Northern Virginia, the key to Confederate military might in the East, remained safely ensconced in and around Fredericksburg. In the West, Union forces under William Rosecrans had driven off a Southern offensive at Stone's River, just north of Murfreesborough. But the South's port of Vicksburg, key to the western theater, seemed unassailable.

The Union controlled much of the northern part of the Mississippi River and the area north of Baton Rouge down to New Orleans. Confederate Vicksburg controlled the middle. Situated on high bluffs above a horseshoe bend on the river, the city seemed almost impregnable. It effectively blocked the shipment of midwestern goods into the North. At the same time, it also allowed critically needed beef and produce from Texas, as well as European weaponry, into the blockaded eastern states. Jefferson Davis knew well the importance of Vicksburg, calling it the nailhead that held the two halves of the Confederacy together.

Lincoln desperately wanted to pry out that nailhead. In the summer of 1862 his flag officer, David Glasgow Farragut, had steamed up the Mississippi with a fleet of warships and demanded Vicksburg's surrender. The Confederate military governor responded prophetically, "Mississippians don't know, and refuse to learn, how to surrender." Farragut steamed back downriver.

Since October, the new commander of the Army of the Tennessee, Ulysses S. Grant, had been worrying over the Vicksburg problem. Another controversial Union appointment, Grant was criticized by some for his battle performance, and there were rumors of his heavy

AN actual sketch, made on the spot by one of the Special Artists of Frank Leslie's Illustrated Newspaper.

Mr. Leslie holds the copyright and reserves the exclusive right of publication

drinking. His superior, Gen. Henry W. Halleck, was looking for someone to replace him and Grant knew it. But Grant also thought he knew a way to get at Vicksburg: overland, from the east. In November he began his move on the port, but he was stymied by the enemy. On December 20, his supply base at Holly Springs was taken by the

Rebels. At the same time Nathan Bedford Forrest and his Confederate cavalry had wreaked havoc on the Union supply route to Kentucky, ripping up miles of railroad and telegraph lines. Though his campaign was thwarted, the tenacious Grant had not given up. Lincoln himself could see that. At one point, when pressed to remove Grant, the

At the Battle of Stone's River outside Murfreesborough, bluecoats charge the enemy on the far shore. The Army of Tennessee, under the Confederate's obstreperous Braxton Bragg, lost 10,300 men here—almost a third of its strength—before retreating.

The Battle of Stone River—
the decisive charge across Stone River Friday Afte...
4° Cl—

— River clear and
rapid —

President replied, "I think we'll try him a little longer. He fights."

For all the South's victories and ardor, as 1863 began, her leaders knew they were not winning the war. Every battle cost men and supplies they could ill afford, and now, with Lincoln's Emancipation Proclamation, they were losing badly needed European support.

The Southern populace, too, was becoming disaffected as deprivation worsened and profiteers gouged them for sugar, salt, flour, and other necessities. Farmers suffered from high taxes and from army impressment agents, who paid them only 20 percent of market value for their crops and livestock. Jefferson Davis, an aloof, somewhat arrogant man,

was unable to rally support for the cause. Though the South's outnumbered and outgunned soldiers fought fiercely and courageously, the only weapon that they could count on indefinitely was their chilling Rebel yell. As one historian explained, "Simply stated, the South could not afford [her] victories, brilliant as they were."

My Dear Wife,

...I see that it takes from seven to ten days for a letter to get through now. I received the gloves all right. They fit me nicely and are just what I want.... You ask me about clothes. That was the cause of my sickness. I was not dressed warm enough and took cold.... I bought me a thick pair of pants and a knit undercoat which I wear under my blouse and I wear a thick knit shirt over my woolen one, so that I am now warmly dressed....

I must close this letter as we are to be reviewed by Genl. Burnside. Thirty thousand men of us. It will be a grand sight. It is warm and pleasant this morning. The roads are good. I have no stamp. You must excuse as I cannot get them. Love to all. Good by.

Yours,

Warm patina marks Halsey's old Colt revolver (below)—the police model favored by some Union officers. Samuel Colt patented the revolver in 1836 but could not convince army ordnance experts of its efficacy until the Mexican War. Ironically, a Quaker—industrialist Christopher Spencer—invented the Spencer repeating rifle (lower). Revolutionizing warfare, the repeaters blitzed battlefields the last two years of the war, pushing casualty figures to unprecedented heights.

Seacoast defenses bristled with multi-ton Columbiad cannon, like these (opposite) aimed at Pensacola Bay, Florida.

Minié balls and other bullets replaced powder early in the war, making loading and firing a far more rapid procedure.

Ironclad navies, machine guns, and hand grenades were among the many military innovations tried out and improved upon during the course of the war. But the invention that would change the face of this conflict, and subsequent ones, was the repeating rifle.

At the beginning of the war, most soldiers were equipped with single-shot, muzzle-loading rifles that required many steps to load and fire. Still, they were vast improvements over the old smooth-bore muskets, because their grooved, or rifled, bores helped put a spin on a

bullet, sending it four times farther than a smooth bore could. A new kind of ammunition was on hand to aid the rifles' efficiency. The fast-loading minié ball—an American adaptation of a French design—could be more quickly loaded than previous bullets. A good man could fire two shots a minute, and the soft lead cylinder of a minié could kill or wound at half a mile, expanding as it hit the bone of its victim.

Breechloaders were another battlefield improvement. One of the more popular had been invented by Ambrose Burnside in mid-century, but he lost the patent before the war and realized no profit on his work. Then came the repeating rifles—the Spencers and the Henrys. Used first by the Union, the repeater was described by Rebels as "that damn Yankee rifle that can be loaded on Sunday and fired all week."

WINTER 1863

❖ **January 11** Northern forces take Fort Hindman on the Arkansas River.

❖ **January 11** The Rebel raider C.S.S. *Alabama* sinks the U.S.S. *Hatteras* off Galveston, Texas.

❖ **Mid-January** Burnside makes plans to march on Lee's army in Fredericksburg yet again.

CAMP BELOW FALMOUTH, VA.
JANUARY 24, 1863

Dear Wife,

The last I wrote you we were just about leaving for a fight

and...it came on to rain and the waggon trains got stuck

in the mud and we could not make any advance and we

have returned to our old camp and shall stay for some

time as the roads are in a terrible condition. I write these

few lines to let you know that I am well and that I stood

the hard march through the rain and mud well....

From your loving husband,

After the Union debacle at Fredericksburg, Burnside continued at the helm of the Army of the Potomac only reluctantly, knowing he had lost the confidence of his subordinates. But, he was still determined to get at Lee.

On the morning of January 20, he once again sent his troops toward Lee in Fredericksburg, assuring them that this was "an auspicious moment" to end the war. By evening, a cold rain was falling, the kind, as one officer noted, "in which courage is worn out...." By dawn torrential rains had turned the roads to mud. All day, men and horses struggled to pull wagons and artillery free of the mire, but to no avail. As Burnside rode the lines, one teamster called to him, "General, the auspicious moment has arrived."

For Burnside it proved most inauspicious. When the rains abated four days later, his infamous Mud March had left his men ill and exhausted, and his military command buried in the mud. The barrage of criticism unleashed on the general came in part from one of his own generals, Joseph Hooker, known as "Fighting Joe." Incensed, Burnside insisted that Hooker and other "insubordinate" officers be dismissed, else he himself would resign. Lincoln responded by replacing Burnside with none other than Joe Hooker.

Battling rain, wind, and mud, Burnside's ill-fated Army of the Potomac struggles toward Fredericksburg in this depiction by well-known war illustrator Alfred R. Waud (right). Unlike war photographers who were limited to still images, illustrators following the armies could capture in telling detail the pain and glory of war.

WINTER 1863

❖ **January 20-23** Burnside's Army of the Potomac attempts its failed Mud March on Fredericksburg.

❖ **January 26** Lincoln loses confidence in Burnside and replaces him with Maj. Gen. Joseph Hooker, who tries to restore the morale of the army.

CAMP BELOW FALMOUTH
JANUARY 28, 1863

Dear Wife,

...It has rained & snowed since yesterday morning and it is very muddy so that we cannot do anything. It is very unpleasant. If you have sent me a box I am afraid that it will not get here untill every thing spoils as the rail road from Aquia Creek has so much to do to keep us in provisions that they will not cary boxes and the roads are so bad that the Quarter Master will not send the teams after them....

The Ford boys sent home $21 dollars. They ought to have sent $40 but would not. I have a list of...the men that sent home their money.... I weigh 165 lbs, am rugged as a bear, all but my teeth. They bother me some....

From your loveing husband,

Hampered by its lack of railroads, the South stumbled along with less than half the North's capacity. Rebel raiders delighted in derailing Union trains (below) and tearing up tracks.

A Federal battery near Petersburg awaits battle. With the advent of railroading, such massive weaponry could be transported with relative ease.

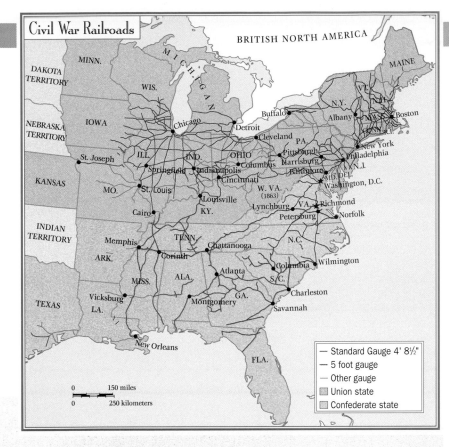

Civil War Railroads

BRITISH NORTH AMERICA

— Standard Gauge 4' 8½"
— 5 foot gauge
— Other gauge
Union state
Confederate state

0   150 miles
0   250 kilometers

With its dedication to an agrarian economy and states' rights, the South had spent hardly any resources in developing a rail system. When war struck, it had only 9,000 miles of track to the North's 22,000. And that was divided between 113 separate, small, and mostly nonlinked lines built to transport crops. When Jefferson Davis attempted to construct a critical link between North Carolina and Virginia, some Confederate leaders cried foul, accusing him of violating states' rights.

Prior to the war, Northern factories had manufactured the South's rolling stock, rails, and spikes. With that supply cut off, the few lines in the South degenerated into decrepit, almost nonfunctional dinosaurs, their trains averaging 12 miles an hour. And without viable railroads, critical supplies could not reach troops—nor could troops, in some instances, reach battles. As much as any other factor, the lack of railroads debilitated the South's war effort. Its only effective recourse was to disable as many Northern lines as possible.

But the North still managed to forge ahead. In 1862 the U.S. Military Railroads Agency was created to facilitate the war effort and convert the many different gauges of different lines into an interlinked system. From April 1862 to September 1863, a West Point-educated civil engineer, Herman Haupt, was in charge of operations. The solemn but tireless Haupt worked the men in his Alexandria rail yard through shifts as long as 16 hours, but his management spawned laudable results. In just 21 days he repaired a vital line to Fredericksburg and won praise from Lincoln, who called one of Haupt's trestle bridges "the most remarkable structure that human eyes ever rested upon."

CAMP NEAR FALMOUTH, VA.
JANUARY 29, 1863

My Dear Wife,

...I want to thank you for the very acceptable present you sent me in the way of socks, cake & tobacco. The pipe from Mr. Thompsons I am now using and it is a very nice one. The cake I gave Charlie a piece of and last night Misters Berry, Stansilo Monise and E. Sturdevant finished it and they all pronounced it good. The tobacco is the right kind...

I am getting along finely now. I have taken in three partners in my mess and Sam cooks for us, which makes it very pleasant. They are all nice men and we can mange to live better where there is so many than to live seperately, and it will be much cheaper for me.... I would like to have some things that your own dear hands had made.... I am glad you are keeping an account of your expenses. It will learn you about doing business....

Yours affectionately,

Hardtack at the ready, two soldiers display the ration most reviled by both armies. No more than water and flour, the biscuits earned such appetizing sobriquets as "teeth-dullers" or "worm castles."

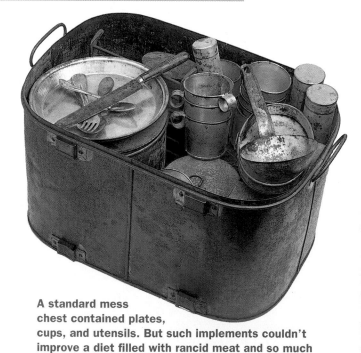

A standard mess chest contained plates, cups, and utensils. But such implements couldn't improve a diet filled with rancid meat and so much grease that one army doctor feared his men would suffer "death from the frying pan."

Union officers relax around their private mess table, while hired servants attend them.

While Confederate soldiers grew ever more ill-fed during the war, Union men savored a more generous ration allocation than any modern army had ever been issued. The daily camp ration for each Federal soldier consisted of 12 ounces pork or 1 pound 4 ounces beef; 1 pound 6 ounces soft bread, 1 pound hard bread, or 1 pound 4 ounces of cornmeal. In addition, men were issued a generous quantity of potatoes, beans, or peas; rice or hominy; coffee; salt; pepper; sugar; vinegar; and sometimes molasses. Early in the war, unskilled company cooks prepared the meals. One soldier characterized the cooks as the most

unsavory soldiers, those "not being able to learn to drill, and too dirty to appear on inspection." Understandably, men often preferred to prepare their own mess, with no better nutritional results. Skillygalee, an economical dish, could be quickly concocted by wetting hardtack with water, then frying it with salt pork. "Hardtack was not so bad an article of food," one soldier affirmed, "even when traversed by insects."

Commissioned officers such as Thomas J. Halsey enjoyed a far greater culinary range. They were given an allowance to purchase supplies from the brigade commissary and had servants to cook for them.

For all ranks of men, boxes of food sent from home broke the tedium of camp food, as did that customary army practice called foraging.

WINTER 1863

❖ **January-March** Grant undertakes his bayou "experiments," building levees and passes, and diverting water to allow his forces access to Vicksburg from the swamps to the north and west of the town. All such attempts ultimately fail.

Sunday Feb 8 th 1863

My Dear Wife

I am tired and weary
this Morning but must ...

**SUNDAY
FEBRUARY 8, 1863**

My Dear Wife,

...I was sitting in my tent by a good fire warming my feet last Wednesday night, just ready for bed, when I heard an orderly ride into camp at a rapid rate and sing out to the adjutant Marching Orders. I hauled on my boots and went to see what was up and learned that we were to march at a quarter past six in the morning with three days cooked rations on some special service. I then had to rout up the cooks and have the meat cooked and see that the men had sufficient ammunition which took nearly the whole night. I got three hours sleep and just as we were ready to start in the morning it commenced snowing and we marched all day through a driving snow storm which made it very hard marching. And just before night it commenced raining. After we had marched some 14 miles we came to a dense pine forest and were marched in to bivouac for the night....

It was a long and dreary night. The worst I ever experienced. They forwarded on to us some liquor which reached us about midnight and that helped us along some. I took a big drink, I tell you, but felt no effect from it as I was nearly worn out....

What we went for I am unable to tell you. It was some secret expedition for some special purpose. I am well this morning and took no cold. I begin to feel like an old soldier and stand it like a hero. I believe this is the first time I have told much of our hardship but such is a soldier's life....

Your loveing and affectionate husband,

Small of stature, John S. Mosby—the Confederacy's Gray Ghost—enjoyed a reputation as one of the South's most daring partisans. After the war, he infuriated fellow Southerners by supporting Grant's Presidency and Reconstruction. Serving as a Justice Department attorney, he later became U.S. consul to Hong Kong.

As the vast armies of the North moved across the war-torn Southern landscape, small, lightning-quick bands of Confederate raiders rode at their heels, nipping and biting at supply lines, tearing up railroads, and generally harassing them. "In no other way," Lincoln complained, "does the enemy give us so much trouble, at so little expense...." The Confederate Congress apparently agreed with Lincoln, because in 1862 it passed a Partisan Ranger Act to encourage guerrilla activity. As an incentive, raiders were to be paid for captured arms or ammunition.

Famous among the irregulars was northern Virginia's legendary Gray Ghost. So effectively did 30-year-old John S. Mosby and his Partisan Raiders harass Union troops moving between the Potomac and Rappahannock Rivers that that stretch of Virginia became known as "Mosby's Confederacy." The raiders would "gather at my call," Mosby said, "like Children of the Mist," then melt away when their work was done.

At war's end some Union commanders prophesied that partisans like Mosby would continue a guerrilla war. But Mosby disdained such talk, saying, "We are soldiers, not highwaymen." Taking off his ostrich-plumed hat and red-lined cape for the last time, Mosby again became a lawyer and went on to serve the reunited country.

Wearing a checkered shirt, Allan Pinkerton, the feisty Scotsman who headed up Union spy operations, poses with fellow agents. Below, a *Harper's Weekly* cover depicts Mosby's Partisan Raiders at work.

WINTER 1863

❖ **February 25** Congress passes legislation that provides for the first national banking system.

❖ **March 3** Congress passes the first Federal conscription act.

❖ **March 8** Mosby captures Union Gen. Edwin Stoughton in Fairfax, Virginia.

CAMP NEAR FALMOUTH, VA.
MARCH 16, 1863

Dear Wife,

...I see by the Papers that the Copper Heads are making quite a stir and may make some trouble but it will not amount to much as I think this Government is strong enough to put them through. Our Regiment had a meeting last week and passed Resolutions of a Patriotic nature condemning the Peace Party and pledging our Lives and all that we have in the cause of our country. There were several speeches made on the occasion, among others, your humble servant. (I do not care to brag, Lib, but as no one but you will see this, one of the bigest men in the Regiment said to me after the Meeting, 'Why, Halsey, did not know that you was so much of a talker.') The meeting passed off pleasantly. The men cheered, the Band played, the Bonfire burned brightly, and alltogether we had a good time....

Your affectionate husband,

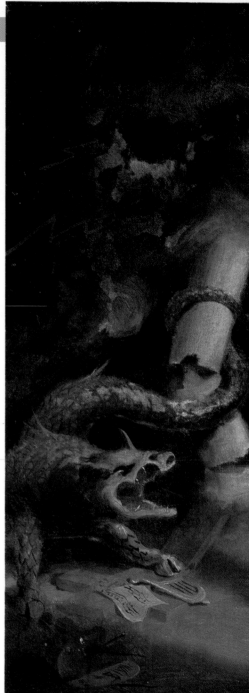

Chained to the Constitution by New York's Tammany Hall Copperheads, a thwarted Lincoln valiantly fights the Southern dragon in this 1862 cartoon. Behind him the capital burns.

As Lincoln and Davis struggle to tear the country asunder, McClellan—the Democrats' 1864 presidential candidate—stands between them.

"Constitution-breaking...negro-loving Pharaseeism of New England." Immigrant laborers in Northern cities quickly joined the Copperheads, but the strongest base of support lay with the farmers of Indiana, Illinois, and Ohio, many of whom had Southern roots. There was even talk of forming a Northwest Confederacy, separate from the loathsome liberals of New England. Copperhead agitators circulated among the troops in the Midwest, advising desertion. Their rhetoric sometimes worked; Grant once had to disband two regiments, owing to Copperhead-induced desertion.

The South watched the Peace Democrats, hoping that their activities would undermine the Northern war effort, or even bring about a negotiated peace. Lincoln, however, was determined to neutralize the anti-war agitators and eventually banished their leader, former Ohio Congressman Clement Vallandigham. Lincoln's stance only added to public rancor. The Peace Democrats were not to be easily silenced. In the elections of 1864, it looked as though the President himself might get bitten by a Copperhead.

"The enemy behind us is more dangerous...than the enemy before us," Lincoln said early in 1863. He was referring to the growing power of the North's Peace Democrats—a groundswell within the party that wanted the war stopped and a peace negotiated. "Copperheads," their opponents called them derisively, referring to their disloyalty and to the copper pins they wore in their lapels. Halsey's letter may be referring to a mass meeting of Peace Democrats held in New York City early in 1863. Decrying the war, their leaders claimed it was "illegal, being unconstitutional, and should not be sustained."

In particular, the Copperheads lambasted emancipation and the

CAMP NEAR FALMOUTH, VA.
MARCH 24, 1863

Dear Wife,

...All is quiet as yet but we are getting ready for a move. How soon it will be I cannot say. Not before the 1st of April, I think. There will be sharp work in every direction very soon. I feel hopeful of the result as I think the Rebels are on their last legs. God grant that we may be successful, as I wish the matter settled. As for a dissolution of this Union, it cannot be and if the South has to be utterly annihilated to crush the Rebellion, so let it be....

We are beautifying our camp with evergreens as if we were going to make our homes here. It looks very beautiful. The men engage in it heartily, each company trying to outdo the other. If I can get a picture taken, I will send it to you. I think you would like it. It serves for a pass time and keeps the men cheerful and contented.

We had an excellent Sermon last Sabbath from some young man sent on by the Christian association and the Col. read a letter from some lady in Newark addressed to the Regiment on those Resolutions we passed here, saying she had an only son in the 11th and she a widow and if she had a dozen she would freely give them in the cause of her country. That, my dear Wife, is true patriotism....

Your loving husband,

Desperate for bread, Richmond women (opposite, bottom) take to the streets, looting bakeries and other stores in their path. Similar riots occurred elsewhere in the Confederacy. In the top illustration, protesting women in Mobile, Alabama, drive back cadets on September 4, 1863.

Entertaining lady visitors, Union officers relax outside their evergreen-bedecked tent. While in winter camps, men often amused themselves by adorning their quarters with boughs of pine, cedar, and holly. Beyond just beautification, the evergreens probably freshened stale tent air with their pitchy redolence.

The privations of war that caused so much suffering on the Southern home front were made only worse by the greed of profiteers. Occasionally, local citizens mounted their own civil war against loathsome speculators, who hoarded food to drive prices up.

The famous Richmond "Bread Riot" began innocuously enough. On April 2 a group of women held a meeting at a local Baptist church to discuss the food shortages, then proceeded to march on the governor's mansion. When the governor offered no consolation, the group—quickly grown to a thousand—took to the streets, shouting "Bread! Bread!" and looting bakeries, jewelry stores, clothing stores, whatever was at hand.

Jefferson Davis himself, with the militia in tow, descended on the crowd and gave it five minutes to disband or the militia would begin shooting. After holding their ground for four minutes, the rioters dispersed. Local newspapers were asked to make no mention of the riot. Instead, the following morning the Richmond *Dispatch* ran a long exposé on "Sufferings in the North." Still, the citizenry had made itself heard. Prices fell somewhat, and the government dispensed more food to the needy. But even harder times were ahead for the capital of the Confederacy.

SPRING 1863

❖ **March 20** Adm. David Dixon Porter summons General Sherman to help free his fleet, trapped in Steele's Bayou, north of Vicksburg, Mississippi.

❖ **End of March** Grant concedes failure in his bayou "experiments" and begins to plan for an overland attack on Vicksburg from the east.

CAMP NEAR FALMOUTH, VA.
MARCH 30, 1863

Dear Wife,

Although I am not indebted to you a letter, I am going to write one as I feel lonely tonight.... I buried another of my boys yesterday...a very nice young fellow. He was taken sick about ten days ago with the typhoid fever. He was about nineteen years of age. I feel his loss much, but oh how much more keenly will it fall on his parents. Truly in the midst of life we are in death....

We are only allowed 20 lbs of personal baggage including the valise and I cannot cary all of my things now. Hooker does not mean to have as many waggons along as there has been heretofore, and he is right, I think.... I have a great deal of writing to do as we have to keep an account with each man and send a Quarterly Statement to Washington of evry article each man has had, and also of the no. of guns and the amount of ammunition expended....

Your devoted husband,

Hooker (right) introduced corps badges (above) to army life. Worn on the hat, the badges became emblems of pride and a way for officers to identify their own men in battle.

In January 1863, General Hooker took over command of the Army of the Potomac, yet another compromise choice on Lincoln's part. Just as vainglorious as McClellan, Hooker was also controversial, with a reputation for hard drinking and fast living. One officer described Hooker's headquarters as "a combination of barroom and brothel." But Lincoln was more concerned with Hooker's overconfidence than his morals, counseling his new

commander in a famous letter to "beware of rashness."

For all the doubts about him, Fighting Joe did well by his men. During his first months in command, he radically improved sanitation and diet in the Army of the Potomac, where disease had become rampant. He also arranged more furloughs and managed to get Congress to authorize the first pay to the men in months.

By early spring his army was in high spirits and fighting trim, ready to take on Lee once again. And Hooker had a plan for that. With Lee's army still encamped around Fredericksburg, the Federal army began a grand flanking movement to draw the Confederates out of the city and into the countryside east and south of town. With characteristic braggadocio, Hooker proclaimed, "May God have mercy on General Lee, for I shall have none."

In mid-April, Hooker's army started toward the Rappahannock and Lee. But heavy rains kept the Yankees from crossing the river for two weeks.

SPRING 1863

❖ **March 25** Burnside, former commander of the Army of the Potomac, is put in charge of the Department of the Ohio, with orders to move into Tennessee.

❖ **April 2** In Richmond citizens loot and riot, protesting shortages.

As the winter of 1863 gave way to spring and Hooker prepared his army for a final denouement with Lee, Grant continued to work doggedly on the long, hard puzzle of Vicksburg. As Adm. David Dixon Porter had reported, "Ships cannot crawl up hills 300 feet high, and it is that part of Vicksburg that must be taken by the Army." But every attempt to get an army to Vicksburg had so far failed. Knowing that Lincoln favored finding a way to come at Vicksburg through the swamps north of town, Grant, though himself skeptical, began his bayou "experiments." Through the winter, as his men suffered from damp, disease, and poor morale, he tried four different canal-building and water-diversion schemes to get his army through the bayous. All of them proved fiascos, and finally in late March Grant returned to his original idea—to bring his army overland from the east and launch an attack on the town from that side.

In a long, daring maneuver, he moved his men from Milliken's Bend, on the west side of the Mississippi north of Vicksburg 40 miles, south to New Carthage, below Vicksburg. Using diversionary tactics and old levee roads for the march, he managed to keep the South unaware of the movements of his 40,000 men. Meanwhile, under cover of darkness, Admiral Porter had to find a way to move his fleet, which was transporting some of Grant's troops, south past the Vicksburg bluffs, so that he could rendezvous downriver with the rest of Grant's army. Porter chose the night of April 16, when the citizens of Vicksburg, he had been informed, would be celebrating at a town gala. But as the 11-vessel Union convoy slid quietly past the Vicksburg batteries, Confederate pickets spotted

it. A few courageous town defenders crossed to the far shore and fired buildings that silhouetted the Union armada. Soon, "the river was lighted up as if by sunlight," recalled Grant's 12-year-old son Fred, watching upriver with his father. Despite heavy shelling, most of Porter's ships made it safely downriver. Grant's plan was under way.

On April 30, Grant began landing his forces on the east side of the river at Bruinsburg and, with William Tecumseh Sherman aiding the plan, began a circuitous, weeks-long march on Vicksburg. First moving his army northeast, Grant captured Mississippi's capital of Jackson on May 14, depriving the South of one of its few manufacturing towns. More important, the Union Army destroyed the rail lines feeding through Jackson and into Vicksburg.

Turning west, Grant now moved

directly toward his goal. By this time the South, well aware of his movements, was putting up a fight, but the Union forces defeated the opposition at Champion Hill and again at Big Black River. On May 18 the Yankees were at the threshold of Vicksburg. The following day they attacked, but as always before, Vicksburg's defenders repulsed them. Grant waited, then tried one more time before deciding that if the "Gibraltar of America" could not be taken by force, it would be taken by siege. With Union artillery bombarding the town, Vicksburg's citizens abandoned their homes and dug hillside caves for safety. As the siege dragged on, food ran low and utter misery ensued. But apparently, as Admiral Farragut had been told a year before, "Mississippians don't know, and refuse to learn, how to surrender."

Fight for the Mississippi: Determined to control the mighty river, Union forces mounted various assaults that took them deep into jungly southern bayous. West of New Orleans, Nathaniel Banks's forces lurk on the shores of Bayou Teche as the Confederate gunboat *Cotton* glides by (opposite). Banks's campaign to take the Teche succeeded—one step in the long battle for the river.

Hoping to elude Vicksburg's fearsome defenses, a convoy of 11 ships under Admiral Porter attempted to slip downriver by night. But when Rebel pickets spotted the ships, "it was as if hell itself were loose that night on the Mississippi."

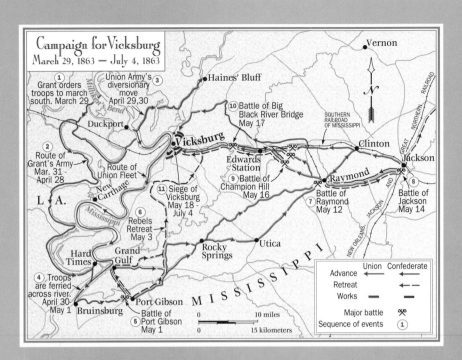

Campaign for Vicksburg
March 29, 1863 — July 4, 1863

CAMP BELOW FALMOUTH, VA.
APRIL 7, 1863

Dear Wife,

I am just in from a grand review of the Army by the President & Genl. Hooker. It was a grand sight. There were about 100,000 men. That is some what of a large number. I never saw anything so grand in my life. The President looks well. He passed through our camp yesterday and I had a good chance to see him. The men cheered him lustily. He had any quantity of officers with him and a body guard of Lancers. They made a splendid sight to look at....

Yours ever,

"Towering genius disdains a beaten path," Lincoln once said, though not of himself. Still, at six foot four, he was a towering genius, standing a foot taller than his noted political opponent, Stephen A. Douglas (top). Lincoln's trademark stovepipe hat only lengthened his aspect. In the above illustration, he wears it to review troops with General Hooker.

A loving, undemanding father, Lincoln delighted in his youngest son, Tad (above). Another of his sons, Willie, died of illness during the war.

Well-wishers thronged Lincoln's Springfield, Illinois, home when, in 1860, he became the new Republican Party's presidential nominee.

Lincoln characterized his frontier boyhood as "the short and simple annals of the poor." But ambition, self-schooling, and a likable style established him as a respected Illinois lawyer and politician. His personal success gave him a lifelong regard for democracy's guarantees. Save for one term in Congress, he had had no national experience before becoming the 16th President.

Considered an antislavery partisan by the South, Lincoln was faced almost immediately with secession. Though plagued by political detractors and incompetent generals, he was determined to return the South to the Union and continue the "great experiment" in democracy. On slavery, he was more ambivalent. Personally abhorring it, he acknowledged that it was protected under the original Constitution.

While abolitionists attacked Lincoln persistently for allowing the national sin of slavery to stand, his Democratic foes castigated him for his emancipation policies. At war's end, he envisioned a merciful reconstruction for the South. In his second inaugural speech, he counseled his countrymen to act "with malice toward none; with charity for all; with firmness in the right." But Lincoln did not live to "bind up the nation's wounds." Two days after Lee's surrender, the Great Emancipator fell to an assassin's bullet.

SPRING 1863

❖ **April 11** Maj. Gen. James Longstreet begins siege of the Federally held town of Suffolk, Virginia.

❖ **April 16** Adm. David Dixon Porter's armada successfully runs the Vicksburg batteries at night, then continues downriver to a rendezvous with Grant's army.

CAMP NEAR FALMOUTH
APRIL 26, 1863

My Dear Wife,

...We are going out this afternoon to be reviewed by Genl. Sickles and the Governor of New Jersey. I do not think much of it. I think more fight & less review would pay better and this Sunday work will not prove a paying institution and it appears strange to me that our head men allow it. Six days shalt thou labor & the seventh rest is a command as binding on the army as on the civilian and I am sometimes fearful that we never shall be successful untill we do better than we have done....

MONDAY 4 O'CLOCK P.M.

We have been reviewed again to day by Genl. D.E. Sickles and the Secratary of State Wm Seward. I presume they are about through and the next thing will be fight. I have got so that I am tired of these great parades. I have seen so much of martial array since I have been out that there is nothing new to me. It was been a lovely day and it would be a grand sight for you at home to see thirty thousand troops with their colors flying, bands playing, with long lines of artillery drawn up in line of battle with hundreds of covered waggons & ambulances with pack mules loaded with ammunition and hundreds of horsman galloping around with their gay uniforms. Oh, the pomp & show of war. I shall be glad when I see the last of it....

Yours as ever,

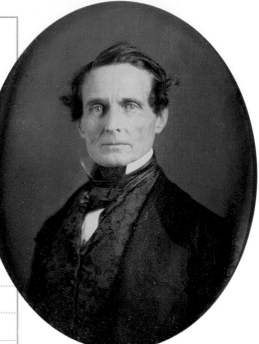

Taken in the 1850s, this daguerrotype captures Davis's characteristic intensity.

In a *Harper's* cartoon, a worried Jefferson Davis peers through a gap in South Mountain during a vulnerable moment for Lee. Unpopular during the war, Davis regained the affections of the South with his postwar imprisonment.

Like Lincoln, Jefferson Davis was born into a hardscrabble farming family in Kentucky. But through the generosity of a wealthy older brother, he received the formal education Lincoln never had, graduating from West Point in 1828. As a young man, he vacillated between politics and the military, fighting in the Black Hawk and Mexican Wars, and serving in the U.S. Congress. In the 1850s he was appointed secretary of war and implemented improvements in the Federal military that ultimately would be used against his own Confederate forces.

At the outbreak of war, Davis, to his dismay, was elected provisional president of the Confederacy. "I thought myself better adapted to command in the field," he stated. As a public figure, Davis was deemed intractable, arrogant, and humorless. Increasingly, the Southern press blamed him for the woes of war and lambasted him for enacting the unpopular measures of conscription and martial law.

Though attacked by his own congress and electorate, Davis persevered. Even after Lee's surrender, Davis hoped to keep the Confederacy alive and tried to escape to Texas. Caught and falsely accused of complicity in Lincoln's assassination, he was imprisoned for two years. He ultimately returned to Mississippi, to die in 1889 at the age of 81.

"Sphinx of the Confederacy," Davis had a hauteur that inspired little warmth or loyalty from his constituents as the war dragged on. But during his 1861 swearing-in at the State House in Montgomery, Alabama (left), optimistic Southerners had thronged the streets, with high hopes for their new leader.

SPRING 1863

❖ **Late April** Hooker begins moving his army into the countryside near Fredericksburg, preparing to engage and destroy Lee's Army of Northern Virginia.

❖ **April 30** At Bruinsburg, Grant's army crosses to the east bank of the Mississippi River below Vicksburg.

CAMP NEAR FALMOUTH, VA.
APRIL 27, 1863

Dear Wife,

Well, here we are yet. I supposed when I last wrote you that we should have left before this time, but such is not the fact. I am all ready to go. My eight days rations in my haversack....

They tease me a good deal about being fat. I tell them it is in consequence of my temperate habits as I neither drink, smoke, chew, or swear. You may think strange yourself at my not using tobacco. It is so much trouble while marching, I took a notion to leave off during the summer campaign....

From your affectionate husband,

I Send you a Piece of flannel which I want marked around the edge with <u>Blue</u> and with red through the center HOOKER. Get a better piece if you can. Get Sue Pruden to make it. Tell her I will pay her for it and hunt her up a nice young fellow for a beaux.

Readying for the inevitable clash between Lee and Hooker, the 1st New York Artillery undergoes inspection. Their 12-pound cannon—called "Napoleons" after their inventor, Napoleon III—ranked as the preferred fieldpieces of both North and South.

Memento of war: a button from Halsey's uniform, now preserved as a family keepsake.

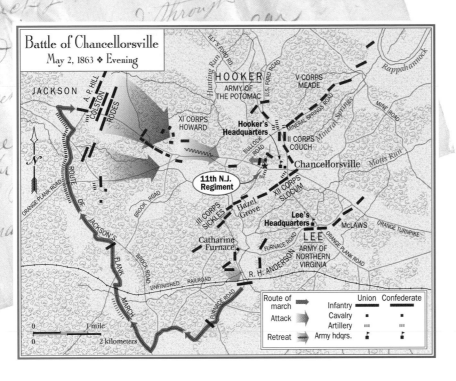

Battle of Chancellorsville
May 2, 1863 ❖ Evening

Route of march	Infantry	Union	Confederate
Attack	Cavalry	■	■
	Artillery	⦀	⦀
Retreat	Army hdqrs.		

0   1 mile
0   2 kilometers

In late April Hooker began his move against Lee's forces in Fredericksburg. Hooker's stratagem called for the Union Army of 134,000 to separate into three units and catch Lee and his 61,000 men in a vast pincer, "where," Hooker proclaimed, "certain destruction awaits him."

Lured off the Fredericksburg heights by the enemy, much of Lee's army moved, as Hooker intended, into the countryside west and south of Fredericksburg. On May 1, Union and Confederate forces met near Chancellorsville, a manor house ten miles west of town that occupied some of the only cleared land in the tangle of woods known as the Wilderness. Lee proceeded boldly against the enemy, and Hooker responded by suddenly and inexplicably losing nerve. Assuming a defensive position, he refused to press an attack against graycoats marching in from Fredericksburg. His officers were stunned, one writing that Hooker seemed "a whipped man."

In contrast, Lee became more audacious than ever. That night he and his brigadier general Stonewall Jackson considered their army's precarious position and devised "one of the biggest gambles in American military history." Defying all battlefield precedent, Lee and Jackson decided to divide the outnumbered Confederate forces and attempt a surprise attack on Hooker's right flank.

SPRING 1863

❖ **May 1** Grant's army marches east from the Mississippi and captures Port Gibson on its way to Jackson.

❖ **May 1-5** Hooker's Army of the Potomac faces off with Lee's Army of Northern Virginia in fighting at Chancellorsville, Fredericksburg, and Salem Church.

CAMP NEAR FALMOUTH
APRIL 27, 1863

Dear Wife,

We are all ready to start and before this reaches you

we shall have crossed the Rappahannock and I hope

we shall have been successfull in our advance move-

ment. The boys are now falling in. I am well & hearty.

It is now five o'clock and we shall march all night.

Good by. God Bless you & the children.

From your loving husband,

No time to write more. Will you soon again. Keep up

good courage and trust all will be well.

James McDavit, one of the 11th New Jersey's "bravest and most promising men."

On the morning of the 3d the contest was renewed, and it was a most terrific fight.... I was shot through the thigh about 9 o'clock, and was carried to the rear by three of my men, one of whom—Sergeant James McDavit, of Dover—was shot through the head and fell dead by my side.... The regiment did splendid work, losing 157 killed and wounded.

FROM A LETTER BY THOMAS J. HALSEY IN HISTORY OF MORRIS COUNTY

Serenity of autumn pervades Hazel Grove (opposite, top), the strategic Chancellorsville hilltop so fiercely contested on May 3, 1863. When Hooker ordered the hill abandoned, the Rebels quickly claimed it and pressed their advantage, driving the Union Army backward (below).

On the morning of May 2, Jackson's famous "foot cavalry" began a daylong, 12-mile march over back roads, while Lee tried to distract Hooker. Union reconnaissance spotted Jackson's column, but Hooker was convinced they were trying to escape. At 5:00 p.m. 25,000 Rebels came screaming out of the forest at Gen. O. O. Howard's unsuspecting 11th Corps, driving it some two miles east. But as the darkness deepened, Hooker's army still held the advantage and a strategic piece of ground— Hazel Grove, an open hilltop that separated Lee's divided army.

At dawn, Hooker again baffled his subordinates by ordering the hilltop abandoned. Confederate forces soon claimed it, and after intense fighting the reunited Confederate Army stormed into the clearing at Chancellorsville. Victory was still not yet Lee's. Two more days of fighting ensued at Salem Church, as Southern forces headed off Union reinforcements pouring in from Fredericksburg. Then on May 6, Hooker retreated across the Rappahannock, leaving Lee with a resounding victory—but one he could ill afford. Though the Union had suffered 17,300 casualties to his 12,800, Lee had little manpower in reserve. And he had lost one man who was, in any circumstance, irreplaceable. Chancellorsville had claimed Stonewall Jackson, Lee's "right arm."

SPRING 1863

❖ **May 9** Joe Johnston, once head of the Army of Northern Virginia, is given command of Confederate forces in Mississippi; John C. Pemberton remains in command of the defense of Vicksburg.

❖ **Mid-May** Grant sweeps through Mississippi, capturing the capital of Jackson and besting the opposition at Raymond and Champion Hill.

Defeated and demoralized, the Union Army retreats back across the Rappahannock River.

CAMP NEAR FALMOUTH, VA.
MAY 16, 1863

CAPT

I thought I would rite you a few lines this evening hoping to find you better, as this leaves me well and hearty. I have been to the hospital to see the boys to day and they ar a geting a long first rate.... I have sent you a corect list of the killd and wounded in our Comp....

I can tell you the Company looks small wen we come out on dress parades. I cant turn out moor than ten file at a time. John Gilbert has been detached at Corps Head Quarters by Special Order No. 73 by Command of Major Generl Sickels to drill team. I think that they had better detach Comp E alltogether and be done with it....

I can make out to get along now, but I want Capt Halsey as soon as he can get back, for I dont know how to make my self contented without you. I heard from Newberry, and he thinks he will be back in two weeks, but I doubt it. Well, Cap, I will stop for this time and rite soon a gain. O, I forgot to tell you that the new recrute came yesterday. He is all right. No moor.

FROM YOUR 2ND LIEUT,
SILAS W. VOLK

Comp. E best respects to you. Rite and let me know how you get a long if you please.

Badly wounded at Chancellorsville, Halsey received this letter from his second lieutenant while recovering from his wounds. He was later taken to a military hospital in Annapolis.

"He lives by the New Testament and fights by the Old," one writer said of General Jackson (top), who fought ruthlessly for the South. When he fell at Chancellorsville, Jeb Stuart (middle) stepped in and brought the Confederates to victory there. Lee's legendary cavalry commander, the flamboyant Stuart, shared Jackson's daring but not his modesty. While at West Point, his vanity had earned him the sobriquet "Beauty." Like Jackson, he too gave his life to the cause, dying a year after Chancellorsville from wounds incurred at nearby Yellow Tavern.

Hunter McGuire (right), a Confederate surgeon, attended the dying Jackson in his last days.

Aided by a full moon, Jackson searches for a way to continue his attack. But Southern pickets mistook him for the enemy, and he was mortally wounded.

Two days after being wounded, Jackson was moved to this bed in a small outbuilding on the Chandler plantation, where he died six days later.

When he was a professor of natural philosophy at Virginia Military Institute, his ways were so odd that his students called him "Tom Fool" Jackson. But after his bravery at the Battle of First Manassas, the eccentric, God-fearing Calvinist had a new name—Stonewall.

The name soon became legend, as Thomas Jonathan "Stonewall" Jackson waged his dazzling Valley Campaign through the Shenandoah in the spring of 1862. In two months his 17,000 battle-weary troops won five battles and diverted the attention of some 60,000 Union soldiers. "Always mystify, mislead, and surprise the enemy...," Jackson preached. But he frequently mystified his own officers as well, keeping them uninformed and thus prone to tactical errors. As one historian observed, the secretive Stonewall apparently "confided in God rather than man."

On the evening after he outflanked Hooker at Chancellorsville, Jackson's brilliant career ended when he was mistakenly shot by Southern pickets. Eight days later, on May 10, he died. His last words: "Let us cross over the river and rest under the shade of the trees."

When news of "Old Jack's" death reached the field, "a great sob swept over the Army...," one major recorded. "It was the heart-break of the Southern Confederacy."

SPRING 1863

❖ **May 18** Grant makes final attempt to take Vicksburg by force. Siege follows.

❖ **June 9** The war's largest cavalry clash occurs at Brandy Station, Virginia.

❖ **June 20** Newly created West Virginia becomes part of the Union.

With the victories at Fredericksburg and Chancellorsville behind him, Lee believed he had "a choice of one of two things: either to retire to Richmond and stand a siege, which must ultimately have ended in surrender, or to invade Pennsylvania." Virginia's ravaged fields could no longer support his army, but the rich Northern farm country could keep his men and horses fed through the summer. And he hoped a victory on Northern soil would also feed the cause of Peace Democrats, who wanted an end to the war. Though Jefferson Davis was skeptical of the plan and considered it ill-advised, Lee prevailed.

By late spring, the Army of Northern Virginia was on the move north. On June 9 Jeb Stuart's cavalry was taken by surprise at Brandy Station, Virginia, resulting in the largest cavalry clash in the war. But at Winchester, the Confederates rolled through a scant Union force.

So fast were the Confederates moving that one soldier maintained he had enjoyed "breakfast in Virginia, whiskey in Maryland, and supper in Pennsylvania." By June 24 the scattered Confederate Army was ranging through the countryside of Pennsylvania and Maryland.

Meanwhile, the indecisive Hooker, still in charge of the Army of the Potomac, was doing little to counter Lee's moves. Finally, at 3 a.m. on June 28, an emissary from Lincoln arrived in Maj. Gen. George Gordon Meade's encampment around Frederick, Maryland, and informed him that he was to replace Hooker. Hooker later confessed to Meade that he had "had enough" of the Army of the Potomac"...and almost wished he had never been born." Meade, though reluctant to assume the command, moved into action quickly, and began pressing the Union Army north along the Pennsylvania border.

At dawn on July 1, two Confederate divisions ambled into Gettysburg, a town of 2,500 people where ten different roads converged. The Confederates were hoping to forage much-needed shoes from a factory in town. Instead they encountered a Union cavalry picket. The encounter might have ended in a skirmish. Instead it drew some 160,000 men into a battle that would shock the divided nation and cost more than 51,000 lives.

By evening the troops of both armies were converging on the town. Though the Union line broke early, it was reestablished, and at dawn the next morning Meade's forces held the high ground, from Culp's Hill to Cemetery Hill and Ridge, to Big and Little Round Tops. Longstreet urged Lee to move back into a defensive position, but the ever victorious Lee ordered attack.

Later that day, John B. Hood's men managed to take Big Round Top, and other Confederate divisions came close to claiming more strategic ground. In the end they failed. Still, Lee would not give up the fight. On the afternoon of July 3, he sent 12,000 men against the Federals holding Cemetery Ridge. Known ever after as Pickett's Charge, the action marked perhaps Lee's worst moment in the war. On July 4, Lee ordered his army into retreat. "It's all my fault," he later said. "I thought my men were invincible." Meade, like his predecessors, did not follow, telling one subordinate, "We have done well enough."

That same day, Grant's long siege of Vicksburg ended with that city's surrender. The tide of war had turned against the South.

"Upon the open fields, like sheaves bound by the reaper...lay the dead," wrote Sgt. Thomas Marbaker, author of Halsey's regimental history. Today, Little Round Top (left) is revered ground to a nation reunited by war.

A bloodbath, Pickett's Charge up Cemetery Ridge cost the South some 6,000 men.

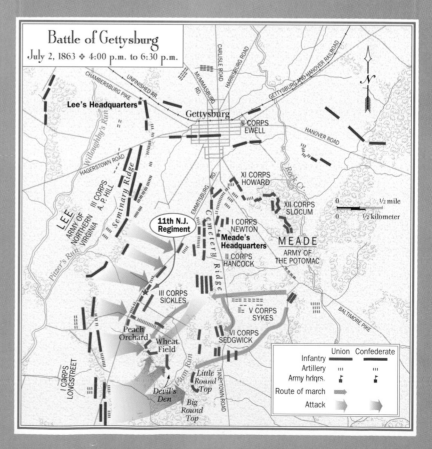

Battle of Gettysburg
July 2, 1863 ❖ 4:00 p.m. to 6:30 p.m.

CHAMBERSBURG PIKE

UNFINISHED RR.

CARLISLE ROAD

HARRISBURG ROAD

MUMMASBURG RD.

GETTYSBURG AND HANOVER RAILROAD

Lee's Headquarters

Gettysburg

II CORPS EWELL

HANOVER ROAD

WILLOUGHBY'S RUN

HAGERSTOWN ROAD

Seminary Ridge

III CORPS A. P. HILL

LEE
ARMY OF NORTHERN VIRGINIA

EMMITSBURG ROAD

XI CORPS HOWARD

Rock Cr.

XII CORPS SLOCUM

Pitzer's Run

11th N.J. Regiment

Cemetery Ridge

I CORPS NEWTON

Meade's Headquarters

II CORPS HANCOCK

MEADE
ARMY OF THE POTOMAC

½ mile

½ kilometer

III CORPS SICKLES

V CORPS SYKES

BALTIMORE PIKE

Peach Orchard

Wheat Field

VI CORPS SEDGWICK

TANEYTOWN ROAD

I CORPS LONGSTREET

Plum Run

Devil's Den

Little Round Top

Big Round Top

	Union	Confederate
Infantry		
Artillery		
Army hdqrs.		
Route of march		
Attack		

JULY 21, 1863
U.S. GENERAL HOSPITAL, ANNAPOLIS, MD.

Dear Wife,

I am now stoping at the hospital in the city of Annapolis....
It was used as a Naval School before this war broke out. The
grounds are beautifully laid out and the buildings are all of
brick and very fine and there are a good many of them.
They are all used as hospitals and filled with wounded men.
The town is situated on Chesapeake Bay and the Severn
River runs right by the yard so that we can bathe & fish, go
a sailing and amuse ourselves in various ways. The town is
pleasantly located, gradually rising from the river and the
breeze from off the lake makes it delightful. This being the
Capitol, the State House is here, which has been built a hundred years. It is the building in which our immortal Washington resigned his commision as Commander in Chief of
the Army of the Revolution, and the city hotel where I put
up was where he had his Head Quarters.

   It is a miserably dull place. There is no enterprise
and I think there is not as much business done here
outside of the army as there is in Dover. There are a great
many Secesh in the place.... With the enterprise that we
Yankees have, it would soon be a flourishing city. Slavery
is its curse. We have an Officers Mess and live quite well
for soldiers....

   I am not very well. My leg bothers me yet. The doctor
tells me it will be six months before it will get sound....

Your devoted husband,

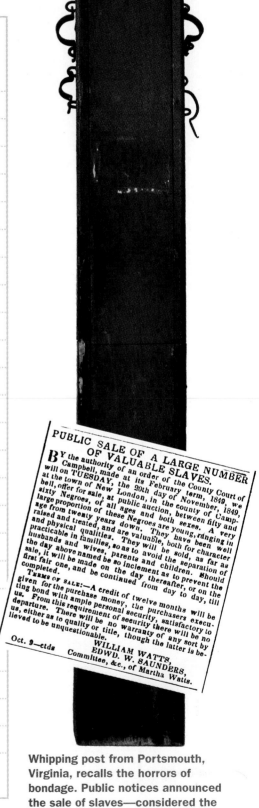

PUBLIC SALE OF A LARGE NUMBER
OF VALUABLE SLAVES.

BY the authority of an order of the County Court of
Campbell, made at its February term, 1849, we
will on TUESDAY, the 20th day of November, 1849,
at the town of New London, in the county of Campbell, offer for sale, at public auction, between fifty and
sixty Negroes, of all ages and both sexes. A very
large proportion of these Negroes are young, ranging in
age from twenty years down. They have been well
raised and treated, and are valuable, both for character
and physical qualities. They will be sold, as far as
practicable in families, so as to avoid the separation of
husbands and wives, parents and children. Should
the day above named be so inclement as to prevent the
sale, it will be made on the day thereafter, or on the
first fair one, and be continued from day to day, till
completed.

TERMS OF SALE:—A credit of twelve months will be
given for the purchase money, the purchasers execu-
ting bond with ample personal security, satisfactory to
us. From this requirement of security there will be no
departure. There will be no warranty of any sort by
us, either as to quality or title, though the latter is believed to be unquestionable.

WILLIAM WATTS,
EDWD. W. SAUNDERS,
Committee, &c., of Martha Watts.

Oct. 9—ctds

Whipping post from Portsmouth, Virginia, recalls the horrors of bondage. Public notices announced the sale of slaves—considered the chattel of their owners.

Bowed by slavery, a family sits outside its ramshackle cabin in Virginia. After the war, life for black sharecroppers in the South often proved little better.

An Atlanta store sells china and glass on one level, slaves on the other. For all its inhumanity, the South's "peculiar institution" survived some 250 years.

The Civil War's figurative line in the sand, the Mason-Dixon Line, originally settled a border dispute between the Penns of Pennsylvania and the Calverts of Maryland. Named for the two Englishmen who surveyed it in the 1760s—Charles Mason and Jeremiah Dixon—it came to demarcate the slave-holding South from the free-soil North.

In the Colonies, slave labor had been a component of both Northern and Southern economies. But anti-slavery sentiments, promulgated by the Quakers, spread throughout the North, gaining ground with the Revolution. As the 18th century ended, the institution of slavery was dying out above the Mason-Dixon Line.

Not so in the states below it, particularly in the cotton belt, where slave labor was essential. In the Deep South's class-based, tradition-based society, an elite core of planters owned half of the nearly four million slaves. Most other white Southerners were small farmers; two-thirds of them owned no slaves at all. But the institution was a part of the culture—one that many observers, like Halsey, blamed for the South's backwardness. Frederick Law Olmsted, traveling in Mississippi in the 1850s, contended that if a planter were asked to point to the benefits wrought by cotton profits "he will point...not to dwellings, libraries, churches, school-houses...he will point to his negroes."

SUMMER 1863

❖ **June** Lee's army moves north into Maryland and Pennsylvania.

❖ **June 28** Lincoln replaces Hooker with Maj. Gen. George Meade.

❖ **July 1-3** Troops clash at Gettysburg.

❖ **July 4** Vicksburg falls to Grant.

William Carney of the 54th Massachusetts
holds the regiment's battle-worn flag.

U.S. GENERAL HOSPITAL
AUGUST 3, 1863

Dear Wife,

...I do not get my strength yet and am fearful that it
will be a long time before I get strong again.... I
think if I could get on to the regiment, I could
resign as I am totally unfit for active Service. What
they will do with me I cannot say or how long they
will keep me here. I wish the War was over as I am
tired of it. I see that my Boys have been in another
fight and I noticed that my orderly Seargant was
wounded and had come on to Washington. I think
my company must be pretty well used up. I heard
that Dave Pruden was appointed a Lieutenant in a
Negro Regiment. Have you heard anything of it....

There are about 1600 Patients here and some
8000 Paroled Prisoners. There was a boat load came
in this morning. I went down to see them. Some of
them were being carried off on stretchers. They
were sick and those that were not sick were dirty &
lousy and looked very bad.... How I pitied them. Oh,
this cruel War. How dreadful it is. I am glad that it is
not being fought on Northern Soil. Those men at
Charleston are having a hot time of it. I think the
South are about tired of it. They do not want to take
their own money at Richmond but are glad enough
to get green backs. Their men tell ours that their
Confederacy is about gone up....

Yours only,

Black troops of the 54th Massachusetts, whose heroics have been celebrated in the modern-day film *Glory*, lead the assault on Fort Wagner, near Charleston. Though it failed, the charge became a noted act of valor.

Members of the 107th United States Colored Troops pose at Fort Corcoran in Washington. "Let the black man get upon his person the brass letters, U.S....," orator Frederick Douglass had exhorted, "Let him get an eagle on his button, and a musket on his shoulder...."

"This Department has no intention...to call into the service of the Government any colored soldiers." Time and again, U.S. Secretary of War Simon Cameron made this reply to the offer of black troops. His stance was dictated by the Militia Act of 1792, which prevented nonwhites from serving in the infantry. But a fever "to fight for the...principles promulgated by President Lincoln" swept through the African-American population, and in July 1862, Congress revised the old militia law. In September, the first black soldiers were mustered into the U.S. Army.

Even with the law behind them, black companies frequently had to fight a dual battle—one for acceptance by their fellow troops and the other against the Southern enemy. When black soldiers who had been slaves were taken prisoner, they were typically shipped back to their owners and sometimes shot. In spite of this, they continued to join up, with some 180,000 serving the Union. Some marched to war with the recognition they deserved. "I know not...where, in all human history...there has been committed a work at once so proud, so precious, so full of hope and glory as the work committed to you," Gov. John Andrew told the commander of the 54th Massachusetts Infantry, a black regiment that would distinguish itself forever on the field of battle.

SUMMER 1863

❖ **July 9** Port Hudson, last Rebel defense on the Mississippi, surrenders. The river is now Union controlled and the Confederacy cut in two.

❖ **July 13-16** Unchecked draft riot creates chaos in New York City; more than a hundred die. Blacks are particularly singled out for violence.

WASHINGTON, D.C.
AUGUST 10, 1863

Dear Wife,

I left Annapolis on Saturday and shall leave for the
Regiment this afternoon. The weather is extremely
hot & it is about as much as I want to do to get about.
I expect to have a hard time of it in finding the army,
but shall try & get to them. My health is now pretty
good. My legs are out of tune & I am fearful they will
give out....

    I should like to have you visit Washington. There
is a great deal to be seen.... If I live to get through
with this job, I mean to bring you down here....

Your devoted & loveing husband,

Col. Robert McAllister,
commander of the
11th New Jersey, was
severely wounded at
Gettysburg. Near the
war's end he was
brevetted major general.

Col. McAllister addressed the Eleventh Regiment as follows: "Sons of New Jersey, the hour of battle is at hand. The soil of Pennsylvania is the contested field. We must stand shoulder-to-shoulder with her sons and drive the enemy from her borders, cost what it may....
    Now with hearts filled with love of country and a firm reliance on God, let us go forward. Are you ready for the march, and the fight?"

FROM *HISTORY OF THE ELEVENTH NEW JERSEY VOLUNTEERS*

From fecund meadow to field of death, the ground near the
Peach Orchard swells with corpses. Confederates cut down
the exposed Federal line here, and many officers and men
of Halsey's regiment fell in the "desperate fighting."

While Captain Halsey was recuperating, his regiment was in the thick of the war. The regimental history, written by Sgt. Thomas Marbaker, records that on June 11th, the 11th New Jersey left the Chancellorsville area with General Sickles's 3rd Corps and began marching northward in "extreme heat" and "stifling clouds of dust." By June 25, they had crossed into Maryland, where they "were welcomed with bright smiles and waving handkerchiefs." But the sense of impending battle hung across the land.

On the morning of July 2, the 11th New Jersey headed down the Emmitsburg Road toward the fighting in Gettysburg. By midafternoon they were deploying near the Smith house. "Scarcely had the line taken position when they opened upon us a terrible fire," Marbaker wrote. The fierce fighting continued through the day, as brigades from A. P. Hill's division bore down on the Union 3rd Corps. The next day the regiment moved about a mile, to the rear of a line of batteries, a position they "held during the heavy cannonading that preceded Pickett's charge." When the smoke of battle cleared, the 11th New Jersey had lost 21 men, with another 124 wounded and 12 missing. Leaving the killing fields and their "pestilential stench," the regiment marched slowly back to Virginia.

In the fighting near the Peach Orchard, Maj. Gen. Daniel Sickles, commander of the 3rd Corps, gallops forward to inspect his line. Meade was furious with him for deploying his men around the Peach Orchard, precariously far in front of the rest of the Union line. Sickles, who lost a leg at Gettysburg, did not emerge a hero.

SUMMER 1863

❖ **July** After the defeat at Gettysburg, Lee's army limps back into Virginia and encamps around Culpeper.

❖ **Late July** Confederate cavalry under John Hunt Morgan begins a raid across the Ohio River. Morgan surrenders at New Lisbon, Ohio.

CAMP NEAR BEVERLY FORD
AUGUST 13, 1863

Dear Wife,

...I shall do my writing to morrow & then assume command of the Regt. as I am the Ranking Officer.... I am fearful that I cannot get out of the service. I ought to have staid at home while I was there but I did not think but what I could get out when I got here. However, as I can ride a horse, I think I can stand it....

I am in hopes that I shall not have to make many more hard marches.... At any rate I shall not untill I get well....

Your affectionate husband,

In a surprise counterattack, New York police manage to stave off rioters at the *Tribune* building (below). But they were unable to save the black man above. Some 30 blacks died in the riot.

Congress passed the first federal draft act in March 1863, and that summer, as the controversial practice of conscription began, riots erupted in several Northern states. But none was as venomous as the conflagration that occurred in New York City in mid-July.

Even though New York's governor, Horatio Seymour, opposed the draft and challenged its constitutionality, the first public drawing for recruits was held without incident in the city on July 11. But rabble-rousers soon made the rounds of factories, inciting the immigrant Irish population. Mostly low-paid workers, the Irish believed that freed blacks would take their jobs, and they had no interest in fighting a war whose results might ruin them.

When a second drawing was held on July 13, Irish workers appeared en masse. A shot rang out and brickbats were hurled through windows. Almost immediately the crowd was out of control, gathering momentum and soon numbering more than 50,000. Burning, looting, and pillaging raged throughout the city. So vengeful was the mob that the *New York Times* dubbed it "the left wing of Lee's army."

After three days of massive destruction, the city resorted to military force. It called in experienced troops returning from Gettysburg, and the rioters were at last overwhelmed.

Looters (above) sack stores throughout New York City, until Union troops put down the crowd with military force (below).

SUMMER 1863

❖ **August 15** Burnside begins the Union advance on Knoxville, Tennessee.

❖ **Mid-August** Rosecrans's Union forces head for Chattanooga, Tennessee.

❖ **August 21** Confederate raiders led by Col. William Quantrill burn Lawrence, Kansas, and kill some 140 civilians.

CAMP NEAR BEVERLY FORD, VA.
SEPTEMBER 5, 1863

Dear Wife,

...Gus Sisco has deserted, it is supposed, as we do not know where he is. Charly Gage was here to see me last week. He is looking well and as patriotic as ever. Lieut. Newberry came back day before yesterday. He is quite lame yet and his wound has not yet healed up. He was foolish in coming back, as when they get one here, he might as well make up his mind to stay, as they will almost let one die before they will let a body go home. We have not heard from the missing men & am fearful they were killed at Gettysburg. How sad for their familes. This war has made many sad homes & will make many more....

I do not know wether I will get a commission as Major or not. I am not going to bother myself anymore with it. If they do not give it to me, I will get out of the army if I can, as I am unable to march....

Your loveing and affectionate husband,

Innovative weapons, land torpedoes—pressure-sensitive mines—added to the horrors of war. After the fall of Georgia's Fort McAllister, Union officers (left) use Rebel prisoners to clear a minefield of unexploded torpedoes.

As with most major conflicts, the Civil War engendered new technologies and political and social change. Below is a list of "firsts" for this nation that arose during the war.

❖ Repeating rifles

❖ Fixed ammunition

❖ Revolving gun turrets

❖ Telescopic sights for rifles

❖ Minefields

❖ First aerial reconnaissance, by balloon

❖ "Aircraft carrier"—for hauling balloons

❖ Anti-aircraft fire, aimed at balloons

❖ Ironclad and steel ships

❖ First black army officer

❖ Military railroads

❖ Military Telegraph and Signal Corps

❖ U.S. Secret Service

❖ Federal income tax

❖ Nationally observed Thanksgiving Day

❖ Conscription

❖ American breadlines

❖ Battle photography

❖ The bugle call "Taps"

Breaking the invidious color barrier, Maj. Martin R. Delany of South Carolina became the first black officer to hold a field command in the U.S. military. A graduate of Harvard Medical School, Delany received his commission in the 104th U.S. Colored Troops on February 26, 1865.

For the first time, hot-air balloons allowed aerial reconnaissance of troops. Prof. Thaddeus Lowe, to the right of the balloon, perfected the technique, beaming his observations back to earth via telegraph.

SUMMER 1863

❖ **September 2** Burnside's forces occupy Knoxville, Tennessee.

❖ **September 5** U.S. minister to Britain, Charles Francis Adams, threatens the British with war if they continue building ships for the Confederacy. The British desist.

CAMP NEAR BEVERLY FORD, VA.
SEPTEMBER 13, 1863

Dear Wife,

...I have not got my Commission yet as Major and I may not get it. I shall not fret over it.... There are to be two men shot next Friday for Desertion. One of them from our Regiment. We shall have to go & see the execution. It will be a sad sight.... It is hard enough to see men shot on the Battlefield. Oh what a horrible thing war is. I shall be a happy man when it is over, if I live to see it.

I had a letter from Mr. Thompson. He informed me that Mrs. Condicts baby was sick and that there was quite a good deal of sickness about the neighborhood. I hope our dear little ones may keep well as well as yourself.

Your affectionate and loveing husband,

"We have got a new Chaplain [E. Clark Cline, above]...and I am in hopes he will be the means of doing us good. There is need enough for it."
Thomas J. Halsey
Sept. 13, 1863

Blindfolded, three deserters from the Army of the Potomac sit on coffins as executioners open fire. High desertion rates tended to reflect an army's likelihood for defeat. Thus, the Army of the Potomac suffered more desertions than the more successful Union forces in the West. From July through November 1863, 592 of its men were tried for desertion, but only 21 were executed.

As the war progressed, the threat of massive desertion struck at the heart of the armies. One in seven Confederates deserted; one in ten Federals. Early in the war, deserters were treated leniently, sometimes just fined but more often sentenced to prison and frequently branded with an ignominious "D." Many men deserted because letters from home implored them to return and help with family matters. Since both sides were more interested in luring back the deserters than in punishing them, Lincoln and Davis periodically issued pardons to all absent soldiers who would return to the fight.

Of the many deserters, only about 260 on each side received the

death sentence, but the executions were carried out with great show. While the brigade of the convicted man formed a hollow square, the prisoner was brought in under guard as a band played the "Death March." Seated on his coffin near an open grave, the deserter was prayed over by the chaplain, blindfolded, then shot by a firing squad. Adding

to the horror, firing squads were sometimes plagued with such poor aim or bad ammunition that they had to shoot several times before their victims finally succumbed. The spectacle made an impression. "I saw a site today that me feel mity Bad," an Alabama private wrote; "I saw a man shot for deserting...thay shot him all to pease...."

AUTUMN 1863

❖ **September 8-9** Bragg's forces move out of Chattanooga, and the Union takes control of the town.

❖ **September 8** Union attack on Fort Sumter is repulsed.

❖ **Mid-September** Longstreet's men arrive to reinforce Bragg.

The Signal Telegraph Train

CAMP NEAR CULPEPPER, VA.
SEPTEMBER 18, 1863

Dear Wife,

Yours of 12th received to day. I wrote you yesterday and after

writing recieved my commision as Major... Col. McAllister

...opposed me in being made Major. He wanted Capt. Loyd, a

brother of his son-in-law appointed. I expect the Col. will be

mad enough about it....

I am grieved to learn of the death of Mrs. Condicts baby & I

suppose you must feel quite sad over it, nursing it so much...

Our folks had a fight here last Sundy where we are now. I

wrote to Mr. Thompson about it & the 5th Corps have been

fighting to day. We can hear the cannonading. We hardly

expect to get in a fight here, although we may....

Your loveing husband,

Source of comfort, the regimental mail wagon kept communications flowing with
surprising alacrity between home and field. When stamps or the cash to buy them
was hard to come by, Union men could write "Soldier's Letter" on the envelope
and have the recipient pay the postage, as Halsey sometimes did.

William H. Loyd initially joined
the militia in 1861 as a
private. By 1864, he had
attained the rank of major.
"That Major Loyd enjoyed the
confidence of his superior
officers is evidenced by his
frequent promotions," noted
a fellow officer.

Even during battle, men of the U.S. Military Telegraph Service strung vital lines that allowed generals quick communication with corps commanders. A total of some 15,000 miles of wire was laid during the war, connecting forts, depots, arsenals, and armies with each other and with Washington.

"Talking torches" made night messages possible but jeopardized the signalman, who became a target for sharpshooters. After the message was sent, a fellow member of the Signal Corps watched through a telescope for a reply.

Rapid field communication during the war relied primarily on electric telegraphy and flag signals. The electric telegraph had been perfected in the 1840s by inventor Samuel Morse, and as the war opened, commercial lines were already in place. Commandeered and quickly expanded by the U.S. Military Telegraph Service, the lines became vital communication links. Since the lines were easily tapped by the enemy, important messages were sent via an enciphered version of Morse code.

It was army surgeon Albert J. Myer who created the flag signal system in the 1850s and who went on to organize the U.S. Signal Corps. Signal stations, established on mountaintops, hilltops, or specially erected towers within six to ten miles of one another, passed messages back and forth. The signalman's tools consisted of seven flags of varying sizes and colors. Choosing a flag that ensured the greatest visibility, he would mount it on a staff and signal. The code, based on combinations of numbers that signified letters, was changed often to prevent the enemy from deciphering it. Though signal communications could be hampered by weather, they enjoyed the advantage of simplicity and mobility. While telegraph lines had to be laid and were easily damaged, signaling required only a piece of high ground, a signalman, and his flags.

AUTUMN 1863

❖ **September 19-20** Bragg beats the Union at the Battle of Chickamauga but does not destroy Rosecrans's army on its retreat back to Chattanooga.

❖ **September 23** Deploying troops on Lookout Mountain and Missionary Ridge, Bragg begins the siege of Chattanooga.

"We are now in the darkest hour of our political existence," Jefferson Davis acknowledged in the summer of 1863. The losses at Gettysburg and Vicksburg had done irretrievable damage to the South, and with the fall of Port Hudson on July 9, the entire Mississippi River had come under Union domain. The Confederacy was now split in two, and Lincoln hoped to divide it even more. Rosecrans, "Old Rosie," his ever-hesitant general in the western theater, had finally launched a campaign in late June against Bragg in Tennessee, forcing the Confederates to fall back 80 miles to Chattanooga.

As the summer wore on, most of Arkansas fell to the North, and in Tennessee, Rosecrans slowly but surely turned his attention to Knoxville and Chattanooga. On August 16, after insistent prodding from Washington, he began a simultaneous move on the two cities. As his own forces slipped quietly into the mountains south of Chattanooga in preparation for an attack on that city's lightly defended side, Ambrose Burnside's army moved on Knoxville, a hundred miles to the north. A haven of Union sympathizers, Knoxville had long been an objective of Lincoln, who wanted to "liberate" its citizenry. The outnumbered Confederate forces in the city gave up without a fight, and, on September 3, Burnside's troops marched triumphantly through the town.

Six days later, Rosecrans telegraphed Washington: "Chattanooga is ours without a struggle and East Tennessee is free." As Bragg's army fled south into Georgia, Rosecrans sent part of his army in pursuit. Along the way, they came upon Rebel deserters who told of a Confederate army in disarray. Their tales goaded the

Battle Above the Clouds, the fight for Lookout Mountain took on mythic proportions. In this rendition, Gen. Joseph Hooker, who later purchased the painting, sits astride his white horse and discusses the coming attack with

Charging cavalry under George Custer routs Rebels near Culpeper, Virginia, where Halsey spent September 1863. Custer made his mark on history more than a decade later, when he took his "last stand" at Little Bighorn.

artillery Maj. John Reynolds. Looming over Chattanooga, the mountain was wrested from Confederate hands in a clear Union victory. "Lookout was ours, never again to be used as a perch by rebel vultures," one officer declared.

Grant, chomping his ever-present cigar, surveys Union-held Lookout Mountain. Though he considered the battle for the mountain no more than a skirmish, the victory there heralded an end to Bragg's siege of Chattanooga.

bluecoats on—just as Bragg had planned. He was waiting for them. On September 19, the two armies met along the Chickamauga, Cherokee for "river of death." In a gruesome and blood-soaked two days, some 35,000 men fell. The battle bought Bragg a rare victory, but he failed to pursue the tattered Union Army as it limped back to Chattanooga to recover.

With Chattanooga still in Northern hands, no real victory had been achieved, as the city was a vital rail and river junction for the South. Bragg positioned his army on Lookout Mountain and Missionary Ridge, at the outskirts of town, cutting off Northern supply lines. Rosecrans seemed incapable of dealing with the crisis, and Lincoln considered the general "confused and stunned like a duck hit on the head."

Lincoln was determined to hold Chattanooga at all costs, and to that end he put Ulysses Grant in charge of the entire western region. Rosecrans was replaced, and Grant called in heavy reinforcements to end the siege. In late November he attacked the "impregnable" Confederate positions. Inspired by Grant's presence, the bluecoats struck hard, driving the Rebels from their positions and securing Chattanooga for the North. With the loss of Chattanooga, Jefferson Davis finally agreed to replace the contentious and inept Bragg, a man whom Confederate cavalry hero Nathan Bedford Forrest considered "a damned scoundrel."

A day after the victory at Chattanooga, on November 26, Lincoln addressed his countrymen on the occasion of the first national Thanksgiving Day. Urging them to be thankful for "the blessings of fruitful fields," he also advised them to "implore the interposition of the Almighty Hand to heal the wounds of the nation."

HEAD QTRS. 11TH RGT. NJ VOLS.
CAMP NEAR CULPEPPER, VA.
SEPTEMBER 26, 1863

Dear Wife,

...Give Paul five dollars...to get me a pair of Major's Infantry Shoulder Straps, <u>regulation</u> size, and send them by mail, as I want them very much.... My wage is now $179 dollars a month & government feeds my horse.... I have good times now. I can ride out whenever I have a mind to....

This afternoon I rode over to Culpepper. It is a miserable looking town. There are some fine houses, but the streets are dirty. There are lots of Negroes and but few whites. I saw a few Secesh ladies out walking....

I tent with the Adjutant—a very fine young fellow. Temperate. Uses no bad language, and is a pleasant companion, and we are first-rate friends....

I am so pleased to think I out generaled the old Col. I expect he will ill use me all he can, but I will not put up with it...as I am to near his equal in rank and ask no favors of him. I worked hard for the position and got it. But I had all the officers in the Regt. to help me, for which I am very thankful. We hardly expect to have much fighting here ...as part of the Army has gone to Tenesee to help Rosecranz....

This is a beautiful night and while I am writing, the different bands are playing and the hills and valley are covered with camp fires, making a beautiful & pleasing prospect. It is very cold nights and the men, being without blankets, hover round their camp fires....

Your affectionate husband,

Union major's shoulder straps

Alexander Beach, Jr., an adjutant for the 11th New Jersey and Halsey's tent mate.

Music helped pass the time during the long days of camp life, spent far from friends and loved ones. Here, a Union regimental band prepares to play a serenade. During battle, the musicians often acted as litter bearers.

Sheet music popular during the war extolled patriotic ideals and Victorian sentimentality.

During the long nights around campfires, the men often turned to song for consolation. Most regiments had someone who could play a fiddle, a jew's-harp, or the bones, and the men indulged in sentimental ballads like "Tenting on the Old Camp Ground," high-spirited ditties like "The Goose Hangs High," or songs that satirized army life, like the Southern favorite "Goober Peas."

The two songs that eventually came to symbolize North and South had checkered histories. The North's stirring "Battle Hymn" was actually set to the music of a Southern camp-meeting hymn. Early in the war, a Massachusetts regiment adopted the hymn's melody for the popular "John Brown's Body." In 1861 New England abolitionist Julia Ward Howe heard the song and claimed that, when she woke the following morning, new verses were "arranging themselves" in her brain. In February 1862 her verses appeared in the *Atlantic Monthly* as the "Battle Hymn of the Republic."

The South's more playful anthem, "Dixie," was originally composed by Northern tunesmith Daniel Decature Emmett for a troupe of blackface minstrels performing in New York. Though the song's verses changed throughout the war, depending on the singer, one part of the refrain never varied, "In Dixie land I'll take my stand, To live and die in Dixie."

AUTUMN 1863

❖ **September 25** Hooker leaves Virginia for Chattanooga with 15,000 Union reinforcements.

❖ **October 9** Lee begins a move on the reduced Army of the Potomac near Bristoe Station, Virginia.

**In Bivouac on Hagamon River
October 12, 1863**

Dear Wife,

...Soon after I had written you the last letter, we recieved orders to go on a Reconnaisance in force to support Cavalry. We were gone three days.... When we returned to Culpepper...the army in motion moving to the...Rappahannoc, where we now are. I have been in the saddle now two days and nearly two nights and feel weary this morning.... The movements of the army are contraband and I, of course, know nothing about what is going on. I only know that we are falling back. Our horses are all saddled and men armed, ready to resist the advance of the Enemy....

**Bivouac near Union Mills, Va
October 18, 1863**

I wrote you last Monday from the banks of the Rappahannock. We are now on the Bull Run stream of which you have heard so much.... We left on Tuesday morning and marched all day and nearly all night. After two hours rest we were again started on the march with orders to allow no man to fall out and to keep well closed up as we must gain the heights of Centerville before the Enemy, and we done it....

It was a grand sight the night we marched. There were fences on both sides of the road and the men would set them on fire and the whole Heavens were lit up. I should think Virginia would want this war to stop. I think Gen. Meade rather got the best of Lee this time as we have got our trains all off safely and have got in a strong position....

Your affectionate husband,

A young Yankee poses in the exotic regalia of a Zouave soldier, fashioned after the French Algerian uniform.

Katharine Prescott Wormeley made the war her own cause. Organizing a woman's aid society, she put the families of Union soldiers to work. Early in the conflict, the ladies produced some 65,000 needed shirts for the Quartermaster's Department. Socks, shirts, and other essentials provided by the home front helped fuel the war effort on both sides.

Cold comfort: During December 1862, a camp in the woods became home for many Fredericksburg families, as bombs from both sides pelted their city. Most residents fled to the country, subsisting on whatever they could find. Here, a soldier bids farewell to loved ones before returning to Lee's army.

Far from the front, Northern families could afford to celebrate Grant's victory at Vicksburg with playful abandon, but the citizens of that besieged Southern city had learned to live in hand-dug caves and to eat cat, dog, and horse meat.

Southerners are "unquestionably the most prosperous people on earth," South Carolina Senator James Hammond declared in 1859. By 1860, the per capita income of Southern whites was 95 percent higher than that of their Northern counterparts. But three years later, those same Southerners could not afford bread to eat.

With no industrial base and little agricultural diversity, the prewar South had relied heavily on Northern manufactured goods, wheat, and corn—commodities that disappeared with the war. To exacerbate matters, a Union blockade prohibited foreign trade, and Confederate currency—"printing-press money"—was worth almost nothing.

As the war deepened, the Southern home front became a place of vast privation. "I have seven children; what shall I do?" a desperate Richmond mother asked of a grocer. "I don't know, madam," he replied coolly, "unless you eat your children."

Northern women, too, had to cope with the hardships of husbandless homes, but the economy was booming. Despite the lack of manpower, mechanized farming produced record harvests of corn and wheat, and factories hummed with war activity. The South's prediction—that the lack of its trade would "make grass grow in the streets of New York"—had proved grossly mistaken.

AUTUMN 1863

❖ **October 17** Grant is appointed commander of Federal forces in the West.

❖ **October 19** Maj. Gen. George Thomas replaces Rosecrans at Chattanooga.

❖ **October 23** Grant arrives in Chattanooga to oversee the defense of the city.

HEAD QTRS. 11TH REGT. N.J. VOLS.
CAMP NEAR WARRENTON JUNCTION, VA. NOVEMBER 4, 1863

Dear Lib,

You will probably guess by the size of this note paper that I have recieved the things

you sent me in Adjt. Beachs box. The box came today & I have eat up the candy, am

writing on the paper & have smoked some of the tobacco you so kindly sent me & shall

read out of the Bible before I retire on my humble couch....

I see by the little note that you have 181 ½ bush of wheat. You can have it ground &

sell a couple of hundred & keep the ballance for your own use as I want some cakes

when I get home. The corn you must sell and it will help pay the taxes. Have you heard

Miller say how much hay was put in stack? It will help you along some. It has cost me a

good deal to equip myself, the most I want now is a new thick coat and I will have to

send on I think & have one made. Rogers & Raymond have my measure & I could write

to them. If you get that coat fixed, you may get some <u>Red Flannel</u>, shrink it before it is

made up, and make me two shirts. I want the bosoms made up in fancy style. You see

that I am getting proud in my old days. I must keep in sight of the fashions....

From your loveing husband,

Uniform of a fallen hero, this pellet-gouged frock coat (near left) marks the Union's first casualty—Col. Elmer Ellsworth. Before he was shot down in Virginia on May 24, 1861, Ellsworth had been a famous prewar militarist, whose drilling Zouave volunteers had thrilled spectators. Halsey, too, had admired Ellsworth and even named one of his sons after the celebrity.

Repaired bullet and slug holes pock the coat of Capt. Joseph Storey of the 43rd Georgia Infantry. Army issue did not keep Southern men in uniform, and soldiers relied on loved ones to send them homemade habiliments. Or they scavenged from Union dead and wounded, disdainfully proclaiming: "All a Yankee is worth is his shoes."

Members of the 114th Pennsylvania sport the exotic Zouave uniform popular during the war. Patterned on the famous French Algerian uniform, the outfits boasted bolero-style jackets, ballooning trousers, and wide sashes.

Early in the war, enlisted men of the Sumter Light Guards wore simple shell jackets while officers donned fashionable frock coats. Not until 1863 were uniforms standardized throughout both armies.

The first volunteers set off to war dressed in an array of elaborate finery. In both North and South, each regiment could express its élan by designing its own uniform. The diversity of outfits was tolerated because, at the commencement of the war, neither army had enough resources on hand to dress its troops uniformly, and so individual states were paid to do the job. But the non-uniformity caused confusion on the battlefield, and by late 1863 the Union and Confederate Armies had adopted standardized uniforms.

In the North men were issued an annual allotment of coats, caps, trousers, and flannel underwear; officers like Halsey purchased their own uniforms. Yankee troops appeared princely compared to their Rebel counterparts, who, as the war went on, often lacked any uniform at all. More fortunate soldiers were sent clothes by their families, others scrounged bits and pieces from civilians, and not a few scavenged uniforms from dead Federals.

Lee appealed desperately to the Confederate government to alleviate his men's ragged barefootedness, but to little avail. Still, he put on a brave show for outsiders. To a British visitor staring at the backs of a parading unit's tattered breeches, Lee said reassuringly, "Never mind the raggedness. The enemy never sees the backs of my Texans."

AUTUMN 1863

❖ **October 27** Union Brig. Gen. William Smith opens the supply route to Chattanooga.

❖ **November 4** Longstreet's forces around Chattanooga are sent to Knoxville by Bragg to attack Union troops holding the town. The Confederates attack and subsequent siege fails.

BRANDY STATION, VA.
NOVEMBER 8, 1863

Dear Wife,

How different I have spent this Sabbath Day from what I should had I been in my quiet home. Instead of going to church, I have been in the saddle all day chasing the Rebels with roar of artillery constantly ringing in my ears, amid the excitement & turmoil of a vast army on the move & flushed with the victorious movement we have made on the enemy. We left camp yesterday morning & advanced to the Rappahannoc. Ours, the 3rd Corps, was to stop at Kellys Farm, the 6th Corps at Rappahannoc Station. We attacked the enemy & repulsed them. Took some three hundred prisoners & killed a good many. The 6th Corps were more successful. They took some 1500 prisoners, 6 guns & caisons, 4 battle flags & some 100 officers with but small loss on our side. The enemy were taken by surprize as they were fixing winter quarters & left fires in their stockades & bags of flour & salt, which they had been cooking, and also new clothing which they had not time to take. The army is in high glee & feel as if we could whip them if they make a stand....

Last night I slept on the ground without a tent but slept warm untill three o'clock when my feet got cold. About three o'clock a Negro came in camp with a fine horse belonging to the Rebel Gen. Rhoads. He was smart. He was an intelligent looking fellow. He informed us that the Johnys were retreating. We get a great deal of information from them. They are the only friends we have here....

Your loveing husband,

Richmond's "Crazy Bet"—Elizabeth Van Lew—spent the war years ministering to Federal soldiers in Libby Prison and passing on information gleaned from them to Northern spymasters.

Confederate cipher disk was based on a 400-year-old European method of decoding.

Confederate spy Henry Thomas Harrison holds a coded missive for his wife. It reads, simply, "I love you."

Brazen espionage ends in gruesome death for two Confederate agents who infiltrated the Army of the Cumberland. The pair tried to pass themselves off as Federal inspector generals working for General Rosecrans. The ploy almost worked before Army officers became suspicious and heads rolled.

Among the memorable characters that emerged from the fabric of war were its spies. Some Northern agents were recruited by Allan Pinkerton, the Union's foremost spymaster; others, on both sides, worked independently.

Perhaps the most flamboyant of these was the South's Belle Boyd. An untamable daughter of the Shenandoah, Belle once shot a Yankee soldier who insulted her mother. But her bravado also provided Stonewall Jackson with information that led to his surprise attack on Union forces at Front Royal, Virginia. Anything but discreet, Belle bruited her exploits

about so loudly that she was dubbed "the Siren of the Shenandoah."

Far more discreet, the Washington socialite and Southern sympathizer Rose Greenhow operated from her home, within sight of the White House. Described by Pinkerton himself as having "almost irresistible seductive powers," the widow Greenhow put these to good use in the summer of 1861, garnering critical information from high-placed Union admirers. Mrs. Greenhow's short-lived career in espionage ended when Pinkerton arrested her in August 1861.

One of the North's most talented spies served in the New York Police

Department before the war. In his 40s, Tim Webster was a double agent who had a fine talent for passing himself off as a Southern sympathizer. In Baltimore he infiltrated a secret secessionist organization, and in Tennessee Southern officers honored him with an official army chapeau. His derring-do at last caught up with him. On April 29, 1862, he was hanged in Richmond.

CAMP NEAR BRANDY STATION, VA.
NOVEMBER 11, 1863

Dear Wife,

...We are now ocupying the Quarters that the Rebels had fixed up for their own use. They had good log shanties built & expected to stay here all winter. But we hurried them out on a double quick. Where we shall go next it is hard for us to tell....

The weather is cold and it freezes now quite hard. Winter will soon be here. How I dread it. I was in hopes the war would end but it does not & may hold out a good while.... The health of our Regt. is good & the Army in good spirits. We have plenty to eat & wear. The poor Johnys suffer a great deal as they do not have the comforts our men do....

From your husband,

One of five holograph copies of the Gettysburg Address, this is the only version that is signed, dated, and titled by Abraham Lincoln.

Address delivered at the dedication of the Cemetery at Gettysburg.

Four score and seven years ago our fathers brought forth on this continent, a new nation, conceived in Liberty, and dedicated to the proposition that all men are created equal.

Now we are engaged in a great civil war, testing whether that nation, or any nation so conceived and so dedicated, can long endure. We are met on a great battle field of that war. We have come to dedicate a portion of that field, as a final resting place for those who here gave their lives, that that nation might live. It is altogether fitting and proper that we should do this.

But, in a larger sense, we can not dedicate— we can not consecrate— we can not hallow— this ground. The brave men, living and dead, who struggled here, have consecrated it, far above our poor power to add or detract. The world will little note, nor long remember what we say here, but it can never forget what they did here. It is for us the living, rather, to be dedicated here to the unfinished work which they who fought here have thus far so nobly advanced. It is rather for us to be here dedicated to the great task remaining before us— that from these honored dead we take increased devotion to that cause for which they gave the last full measure of devotion— that we here highly resolve that these dead shall not have died in vain— that this nation, under God, shall have a new birth of freedom— and that government of the people, by the people, for the people, shall not perish from the earth.

Abraham Lincoln.

November 19, 1863.

The carnage created in the national psyche by the Battle of Gettysburg was mirrored in the carnage spread across the Pennsylvania landscape. Once rich farm fields were strewn with the bodies of thousands of men and horses. Mass graves were quickly filled with the decomposing corpses. An interstate commission was formed and submitted a design for a vast graded cemetery, where the slain were to be reburied with comrades from their own state.

Before the reburials were completed, a ceremony took place to dedicate the hallowed ground. One of the most revered speechifiers of the day, Edward Everett, was asked to deliver the oratory. Lincoln was to be on hand simply to add "a few appropriate remarks."

On November 19, a crowd estimated from 10,000 to 20,000 people gathered for the dedication. In a style appropriate to that period, Everett held forth for two hours. When Lincoln rose, he spoke in his high-pitched voice for only three minutes. The crowd responded with weak applause, but history was more generous. Lincoln's Gettysburg Address has echoed down the decades, having changed forever the meaning of the United States. In place of a loose plurality of states that tolerated slavery, Lincoln

Pilgrims inundate Gettysburg for the dedication of the national cemetery. When Lincoln spoke that day, his words redefined the nation.

insisted that the founding fathers had envisioned a single nation, "conceived in Liberty, and dedicated to the proposition that all men are created equal."

AUTUMN 1863

❖ **November 10** Lee ends his inconclusive Bristoe Campaign against the Army of the Potomac and withdraws to the Rapidan River.

❖ **November 19** Lincoln delivers his Gettysburg Address.

HEAD QTRS. 11TH REGT. N.J. VOLS.
CAMP NEAR BRANDY STATION, VA.
NOVEMBER 24, 1863

My Dear Son,

...I am anxious that you should get a good education & live to grow up & become a

useful member of Society and to do that, you must be a good boy. Be kind to your

mother. Do all you can for her. Remember that you are a soldier's son & that in

your father's abscence you must fill my place....

I suppose you would like to see your Pa. I am certain that I want to see you all &

I suppose you would like to see my horse. He is a very fine one. If my life is spared

to get through this war, I shall keep a horse & then you can learn to ride & drive....

Your affectionate & loveing father,

Contrabands gather at Fort Monroe, Virginia, on their way to work. As the war progressed, many slaves fled their masters and made for the closest Federal haven. Unsure of what the future held for them, they were willing to risk uncertainty for freedom.

Virginia's City Point wharf (opposite) teems with wartime vigor during Grant's siege of nearby Petersburg. By controlling access along the James River and rail lines into the area, the Union Army comfortably wintered 1864, even while deep in enemy territory.

Almost as bedeviling as the enemy itself were the logistics required to field an army of thousands. Keeping men and horses in food alone required elaborate arrangements and carefully guarded supply routes. More than once, battle plans went awry when supply routes were cut off by the enemy.

To complicate matters, Union quartermasters faced a unique problem: how to provide not only for their troops but also for the thousands of contrabands—former slaves—that followed after the liberating armies. In the contraband camps, black families that had escaped one form of suffering now faced many others—exposure, malnutrition, disease. Hearing of their plight, Northern philanthropic organizations hurried medicine, teachers, and other assistance south. Mostly New Englanders with strong abolitionist beliefs, the emissaries worked hard to educate, and instill a sense of independence in, the new freedmen.

By 1863, the army itself had come up with some solutions to the contraband dilemma. "Home farms," where many freedmen could support themselves, were established; some were even paid to grow cotton in the very fields they had worked for former masters. But true independence—a concept not easily imagined by people who had spent their lives in bondage —would be decades in coming.

AUTUMN 1863

❖ **November 20** Sherman arrives with reinforcements in Chattanooga.

❖ **November 23-25** In the Battle of Chattanooga, Union forces rout Confederates holding Missionary Ridge and Lookout Mountain.

ear Wife

near Brandy Station Va Dec 5 1863

Yours of the 22 I recd last

ht and am disappointed

Dear Wife,

Yours of the 22 I recd. last night and am disappointed in not hearing from you since. I am almost used up from our last campaign. It was very cold and I slept out doors what little time I did sleep. One night, the night after the battle, we were on the front line & had neither fire or blankets & we suffered from the cold. There were several perished on the picket line on Sunday night. I suppose you have seen the account of the fight in the papers, so there is no use of my telling you about it. The balls flew rather thick to make it pleasant. Thanks to a kind Providence, I escaped unhurt.

There was no Officers hurt in our Regiment, the killed in my old company was Chas. Mann from Lambertsville. He is the third & last son killed in this war. The wounded were A. P. Lyon from Longwood & Joshua Beach from Rockaway who was taken prisoner. I fear he will die as he was shot in the head & we could no bring him off the field, as we …came near being taken prisoners. When we did leave, you may rest assured we got out of there in a hurry. We rallied the Rgt. in the rear of a Battery & they gave the Rebs grape & cannister, which sent them back faster than they came. We regained our position & buried our dead & brot off our wounded. It was a pretty sharp fight & a hard campaign— eight days & nights constant marching & fighting. We are now expecting to march again. We think to the rear to take up winter quarters....

All my heart to you, my own sweet wife,

In the fall of 1863, Lee and Meade, both back in northern Virginia, danced around one another in a series of moves and countermoves that produced no major battle. Lincoln, as always, disappointed in his general, said that Meade's tactics put him in mind "of an old woman trying to shoo her geese across a creek."

In fact, it was across a creek that Lee and Meade finally met in late November. Meade had learned that Lee's army numbered only half

A. R. Waud.

Meade, at left, meets with portly Maj. Gen. William French, whose delays probably cost the Union a victory at the Mine Run debacle.

the force of his, and he determined to move quickly against it. But Lee detected the Union advance and prepared to meet it. On November 27, fighting erupted in the fields and woods outside the settlement of Locust Grove. Though it was inconclusive, it slowed the Federal advance.

Taking full advantage of the lull, Lee commandeered a ridge behind Mine Run and dug in, creating a formidable seven-mile line. Biting cold

and rain hounded the troops, as the two forces eyed each other across the lines. Union men, knowing that attacking Lee on such well-fortified high ground would be suicide, prepared to die.

Reluctantly, Meade agreed and ordered a withdrawal. His critics, he knew, would lambaste him, because, as he put it, they believed it "better to strew the road to Richmond with the dead bodies of our soldiers than that there should be nothing done."

AUTUMN 1863

❖ **November 26- December 1** Meade moves on Lee's forces at Mine Run but finds their position too strong.

❖ **December 1** Bragg resigns as commander of the Army of Tennessee.

DOVER
DECEMBER 20, 1863

DEAR HUSBAND,

...It is Sunday evening. 8 o'clock. The children are a bed. Burt is a sleep on the lounge a waiting for me to get ready for bed. It is very cold and has the appearance of a snow storm. You can immagine me very lonesome, all alone with the children. I will have an other girl as soon as I can get one.

You write me you want me to fix up. I shall have to commence as I have not got me nothing new this winter. I think I will be ready to go with you everywhere. You may be sure I will stick as close as a <u>tick</u>. You ask me about the furs. I have not got them. Am waiting for you. I have got the cloth for me a cloak. It is cheap. I am sorry I did not get better & if Mr. Lindsley will change it, think I will get a better one as a good one will only cost me 15 dollars. The one I have cost me 9. Most every one thinks I was foolish not to get a better one but, Jeff, everything cost so much. I have just paid Mr. Wighton $22 for stove and repairing room, stove, fixing roof, and doing a little mending. A pretty good bill. Have paid the tax and paid for a tub of butter 12 dollars, 30 cts, 30 cts a pound. It is selling now for 32, 33.... Pork is high and they tell me it will be higher....

The draft begins to call hundreds to Morristown to get exempts. The cars are full all the time. Halsey says it will ruin him if he has to go. He will have to throw up his business and all together he thinks he can't stand it.... I have...sent a hat to Charlie Gage for his mother. Will you please give to him when you see him.... I would like to send you a Christmas Cake....

The baby creeps. He is a smart little fellow. He has a bad cold, other ways the children are all well and I to am over my cold. Hopeing soon to hear from you I will bid you good night from ever loveing and devoted wife,

SARAH E. HALSEY

Wheel of fortune, this lottery spinner from Delaware was filled with the names of Army-eligible men. Officials spun such wheels (left), then reached in and randomly extracted the names of the unlucky chosen. Never a popular government procedure, the draft caused riots in several states.

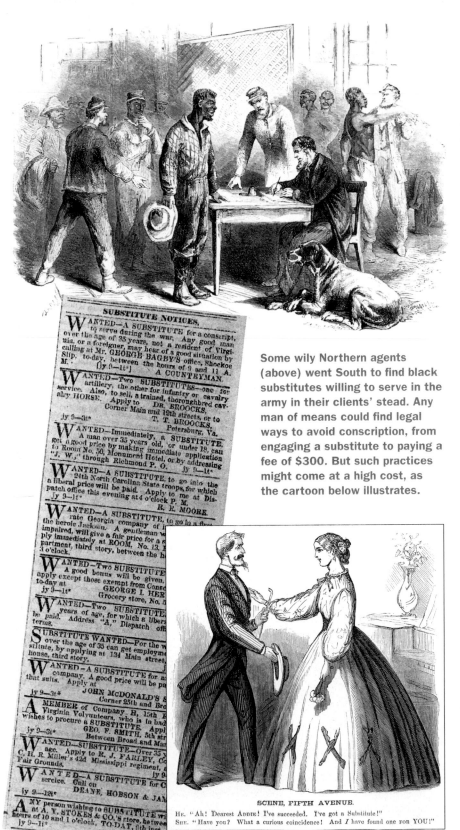

Both North and South surged into war with armies of volunteers committed to the fight. But by April 1862 volunteers were not enough to fuel the Confederate cause, and the first conscription in American history began. Every able-bodied white man between 18 and 35 was subject to the draft. By 1864 desperate for manpower, the Confederate Congress voted to extend the age from 17 to 50 and to include free blacks and slaves for auxiliary service.

The North, with a population almost two and a half times that of the South, was able to wait until March 1863 before passing the Enrollment Act. It required each state to fill a quota whenever new troops were called up. Because conscription was so despised, local jurisdictions offered bounty money to entice men to volunteer. Soon, legions of unscrupulous "bounty jumpers" were enlisting in one jurisdiction, deserting, then joining up again in another.

A commutation clause in the draft laws of both the North and the South allowed men who could afford it to pay $300 instead of enlisting or to hire a substitute. Even more divisive, Confederate men owning or overseeing 20 or more slaves were exempt from service. Such exceptions gave rise on both sides to bitter cries, such as "rich man's war, poor man's fight."

Some wily Northern agents (above) went South to find black substitutes willing to serve in the army in their clients' stead. Any man of means could find legal ways to avoid conscription, from engaging a substitute to paying a fee of $300. But such practices might come at a high cost, as the cartoon below illustrates.

SUBSTITUTE NOTICES.

SCENE, FIFTH AVENUE.

HE. "Ah! Dearest ADDIE! I've succeeded. I've got a Substitute!"
SHE. "Have you? What a curious coincidence! And I have found one FOR YOU!"

AUTUMN 1863

❖ **December 8** Lincoln proposes a Reconstruction policy allowing seceded states to return to the Union if a tenth of their 1860 voters form a pro-Federal government. The plan meets opposition in Congress, whose members feel they have jurisdiction over Reconstruction.

CAMP 11TH N.J. VOLS.
DECEMBER 21, 1863

Dear Wife,

...I think I shall get home

about the sixth of January.

I shall try to get away

about that time. I could get

away sooner, but want to

get my pay as I go through

Washington. I hope you

will get a girl, as I want

you to visit with me as I

would not like to stay

home all the time. There is

nothing new with us & I

am tired of doing nothing.

Time hangs heavy on my

hands.... Burt wrote he

wanted a sett of dominoes.

I will get them for his

Christmas present & shall I

get Frank a drum? As to

Ella, I do not know what to

get her. Will you wait untill

I get home or will you get

her something? Do as you

think best.

Your ever loveing
and devoted husband,

Sea of green swells the Brandy Station countryside around Farley, a manor house used by several commanders as headquarters.

During the winter of 1863-64, General Meade quartered his army around Brandy Station, where the cavalries of North and South had met head-on the previous summer. But that winter a vast city of tents and huts housing 100,000 men covered 10 square miles of the rolling Virginia Piedmont. Just across the Rapidan River, Lee encamped his own ragtag troops.

But all was quiet on the front through the long, cold months, the opposing pickets even greeting each other across the lines. Boredom and homesickness, more than battle, wearied the men. One Union colonel wrote, "This is everywhere the way of war; lie still...then up and maneu-ver...then a big battle; and then a lot more lie still."

The big battle was surely on its way, and in the spring the Federal Army decamped Brandy Station. Its supply train stretched 60 miles, and 6,000 wagons escorted it. Lee had nothing like those resources left, and, knowing that, Grant set in motion the endgame of the war.

Today, Brandy Station, like other Civil War sites, has become a new battleground. A rural hamlet in the midst of farm fields, it is being fought over by developers, who want to commercialize it, and history lovers, who want to preserve a place "where young men died for a cause."

Whiling away a winter's day, Union men at Brandy Station play cards, read newspapers—anything to break the tedium of camp life. Soldiers made the best of it, "logging up" their tents to keep warm and drilling hard. "Mud, mud, is the order of the day here," one officer wrote. "Splash, splash, we go all day."

WINTER 1864

❖ **January 19** In Arkansas an anti-slavery constitution is adopted.

❖ **February 14** Meridian, Missis-sippi, falls to Federal forces.

❖ **February 17** The Confederate submarine *Hunley* sinks the U.S.S. *Housatonic* off Charleston.

DECEMBER 27, 1863
CAMP NEAR BRANDY STATION

Dear Wife,

...I staid in a house last night & had a good bed. The first time in five months. I have not much to write you. I am well & hope soon to see you. The Col. will be home on Tuesday next & then it will not be long untill I can get a leave. You need not answer this as it may not reach me. Love to yourself & the children.

Your devoted husband,

Spit-and-polish soldiers of the 8th U.S. Infantry line up in regulation uniform (bottom). In contrast, Rebel troops (top), desperately in need of clothing, strip uniforms from fallen Union men. Southern soldiers wore just about anything they could find. With little food, clothing, or munitions to support their fight, desertion tempted more and more Confederates.

Two and a half years of war had devastated the Confederacy's resources—its lands, manpower, and matériel. In six of the major battles fought in 1862-63, the South had sustained staggering losses—some 89,000 casualties to the North's 69,000. As 1864 began, its armies had dwindled to only 280,000 men, while Northern armies numbered roughly 600,000. In February Lincoln issued a call for another 500,000 recruits. The South had no such option; there were few white, army-age men left to call.

While his troops spent the long, cold winter of 1863-64 near Brandy Station, Lee pleaded with the government in Richmond for more supplies, food, and clothes for his men, "thousands of whom are barefooted...and nearly all without overcoats, blankets or warm clothing." The sought-after supplies were not forthcoming, in part because the resources were simply lacking and in part because the South had no effective rail system by which to transport them. But a larger problem—one that ultimately derailed the Southern war effort—was also at work. The Confederacy, with its "religion" of states' rights, simply refused to act in concert. As Lee's half-clad army shivered in the cold, North Carolina's governor, Zebulon Vance, hoarded thousands of Confederate uniforms—in the event his own state's regiments might some day need them.

WINTER 1864

❖ **February 20** Publication of circular by Kansas Senator Samuel C. Pomeroy calls on Republicans to name Secretary of Treasury Salmon Chase instead of Lincoln as their presidential candidate.

❖ **March 3** Brig. Gen. Judson Kilpatrick and Col. Ulric Dahlgren's raid on Richmond fails. Dahlgren dies in the fight.

In March 1864, official Washington greeted the new hero of the North—Ulysses S. Grant. Believing he had at last found a general that would lead the Union to victory, Lincoln had appointed the 41-year-old Grant lieutenant general, a rank conferred only on two other men before him—George Washington and Winfield Scott. Grant was now in charge of all Union armies, and, pragmatist that he was, he had a plan. As Lincoln had long urged, Grant would order the Federal armies to act in concert, pressing the enemy at once on all fronts.

In Georgia, Grant's unfailing major general, William Tecumseh Sherman was "to move against Johnston's army, to break it up, and to get into the interior of the enemy's country as far as you can, inflicting all the damage you can against their war resources." Grant's orders to Meade were simpler: "Lee's Army will be your objective point. Wherever Lee goes, there will you go also." At the same time, Benjamin Butler's forces on the Virginia Peninsula were to move on Richmond from the southeast, while Franz Sigel took control of the Shenandoah Valley. In Louisiana, Nathaniel Banks's target was to be Mobile, Alabama.

Grant's own eyes were fixed on Lee's army, and he moved his headquarters to the field with Meade, where he could direct operations personally. Meade, for his part, "was much pleased with Grant. You may rest assured he is not an ordinary man," he told his wife. The men did not warm as quickly to this unknown "savior." He may have bested the Rebels in the West, but, as officers bluntly told Grant, "You have not faced Bobby Lee yet."

But Grant faced a problem potentially more dangerous than Lee. The men who had enlisted at the war's beginning had served the required three years. Soon, nearly half of the Federal forces would be eligible for discharge. Enticing men to stay on, the government offered month-long furloughs and cash bonuses. Ultimately, over half of those up for discharge chose to continue the fight.

In May, Grant's strategy began to unfold, as Sherman pressed Johnston's army, shoving it back toward Atlanta. Faced with a combined Union force of 100,000 men to his 65,000, Johnston perpetually retreated, to the discouragement of his men. By midsummer, Sherman was within 30 miles of Atlanta, having suffered only negligible casualties compared to those sustained by Grant's army in the killing fields of Virginia—the Wilderness, Spotsylvania, Cold Harbor. Grant now knew too well what it was like to face Bobby Lee.

By midsummer, Grant "the savior" had become Grant "the butcher," a trail of blood stretching behind his army. In the battles fought between May 5 and June 12, 1864, he had lost 45 percent of his army, a breathtaking 55,000 casualties. Hundreds of them had been officers, and the Army of the

In an attempt to circumvent a Confederate-held stretch of the James, black soldiers under Benjamin Butler labored 20 weeks to dig a canal at Dutch Gap. Crossing a horseshoe bend in the river, the canal, 174 yards long and 43 yards wide, required removing nearly 67,000 cubic yards of dirt. Steam dredges were used for the final excavating, and in April 1865 the canal was opened to river traffic. Though too late for the war effort, the Dutch Gap Canal did become part of the shipping channel on the James.

Potomac faced a devastating loss of leadership. Yet Grant never wavered in his pursuit of Lee. "That man will fight us," Confederate General Longstreet predicted, "every day and every hour till the end of the war."

In June, Lincoln addressed a nation convulsed by doubt, anger, and anguish. Acknowledging that even "the heavens are hung in black," he nonetheless insisted that this "terrible war" was being waged for a just cause, "national authority over the whole national domain...and the war will end when that object is attained."

MARCH 11, 1864

Dear Wife,

I am ready & shall leave for Washington in the morning
with a lot of men. Will be back on Tuesday if all is well and
then I am in hopes to get home....

I am afraid that I shall have a stormy time. It is raining
hard now. While I am writing this. I can imagine you
putting our little ones to bed & oh how I would like to kiss
them good night & you too. However, I hope soon to see you.

So good night my loved one,

Mary Custis, Lee's wife and daughter
of George Washington's adopted son,
enjoyed a privileged upbringing at her
family's Arlington House mansion. In
later years (below), she suffered war,
ill health, loss of her home, and years
without her husband.

Astride Traveller, Lee attempts to lead the charge
at the Wilderness, as his men force him to safety
in the rear. "I would charge hell itself for that old
man," one soldier declared.

"I walk alone with my thoughts," Lee wrote. Here, the general is flanked by a son (left) and an aide. Lee lost the war, but not his dignity. At Appomattox, he dressed in his best uniform, wearing—it is believed—the gauntlets below.

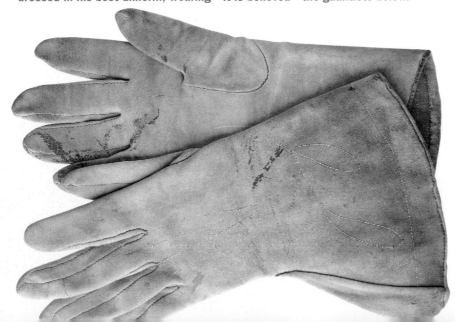

"**H**e loved us like a father and led us like a king.... We trusted him like a providence and obeyed him like a god," a Confederate veteran said of Lee. By sheer virtue of personality, "Uncle Robert" kept afloat the under-fed, underpaid, under-equipped Confederate Army. Lee's military prowess had been well established before the war. As a colonel in the U.S. Army, he was so admired that Lincoln offered him command of the Union forces in 1861. Lee declined, even though he decried secession and considered slavery "a moral and political evil." "I cannot raise my hand against my birthplace, my home, my children," he declared. Instead, he became commander-in-chief of Virginia's forces, but his first year was undistinguished. Not until he repulsed McClellan's forces in the Seven Days' Battles for Richmond did he establish his reputation for invincibility.

Courtly, with a laconic wit off the battlefield, he was, as one of his subordinates proclaimed, "audacity personified" on the field of battle. His audacity may have shed more blood—for both sides—than was necessary. Still, he remained the South's unimpeachable hero. After the war, he counseled reconciliation among his countrymen and spent his last years quietly as president of Washington College, in Lexington, Virginia. But the weight of war had cost him his health. Five years after Appomattox, he died of heart disease.

SPRING 1864

❖ **March 9** Ulysses S. Grant is given the rank of lieutenant general in charge of all U.S. armies.

❖ **March 9** Henry Halleck becomes Grant's chief of staff.

❖ **March 18** Sherman becomes Union commander in the West.

A man of plain talk and simple tastes, "Sam" Grant contended that life was "too brief to be frittered away with explanations." While other commanders worried or raged in the heat of battle, Grant whittled. "The concentration of all that is American," his comrade, writer Theodore Lyman, called Grant.

My Dear Wife,

...My health is <u>good</u>. I am only heart sick but will get over that. You wished to know if Mr. Bassinger said anything to me about coming back. Yes he did and wanted me very much and I made up my mind at one time to stay at home & wish now that I had, as I am not needed here. The Regt. is so small that there is no need of so many officers. However, I will now make the most of it and trust that I will get home again....

I am not sorry that Miller did not take the farm as it is the best investment that I could have, as I think there will be a grand smash up some of these days & real estate is safe.... You see, Dear Wife, that money does not make happiness. If I live to get home again, I think that I shall be the most happy person in the county. My dear wife, I do not want to worship you, but I must say that I fear that I think to much of you & my prayer is that I may be spared to see you again....

I think I told you that I had bot me a fine horse & am well rigged for the campaign that is about to commence. I will write to you often as it relieves me to write to you & I am so glad to get a letter from you. I shall have no other correspondent except the Dr. folks. I must write to them once in a while. It is quite cold down here, yet we can see snow on the Blue Mountains & untill that is gone, the weather will not be pleasant....

Your loveing & affectionate husband,

Cincinnati, Grant's favorite horse, was given him by an admirer after the Battle of Chattanooga.

The "most modest...most honest man I ever knew, with a temper that nothing could disturb," Charles Dana, assistant secretary of war, said of Ulysses Grant. Only five feet eight inches tall and 135 pounds, Grant nonetheless had a gravity that commanded respect—and a determination to fight that finally guaranteed the survival of the Union.

Born in Ohio to a leather tanner, Grant attended West Point and served as a quartermaster in the Mexican War. But a weakness for drink that would periodically haunt him forced him to resign his commission in 1854. After a failed attempt at farming, Grant went to work in his father's Galena, Illinois, leather store. When the war com-menced, he joined up as a colonel and quickly established himself as a fighter. In 1863, "Unconditional Surrender" Grant was given command of the Union forces in the West. Five months later, at the age of 41, he was promoted to lieutenant general in charge of all Union armies.

Better suited to military than political leadership, Grant did not distinguish himself during his two-term Presidency after the war. Diagnosed with throat cancer at the age of 62, he spent his last year working on his acclaimed *Memoirs*. "I think I am a verb instead of a personal pronoun," he wrote in his final days. "A verb is anything that signifies to be; to do; or to suffer. I signify all three."

Though a devoted family man, Grant was forced by economics and war to spend years away from his wife and confidante, Julia, and their four children. On his nomination to the Presidency, the 46-year-old Grant spoke simply and eloquently. "Let us have peace," the former warrior told the war-scarred nation.

SPRING 1864

❖ **Mid-March-May** Union forces engage in the Red River Campaign.

❖ **April 12** Forrest's cavalry captures Fort Pillow, north of Memphis. His troops are accused of atrocities.

❖ **April 17** Grant halts routine prisoner exchanges.

HEAD QUARTERS, 11TH REG. NEW JERSEY V.R.
CAMP NEAR BRANDY STATION, VA.
APRIL 26, 1864

Dear Wife,

...I suppose you are anxiously expecting a movement of the Army. I thought last week that we should have left before this time, but things do not appear to be ready yet. You may remember that it will soon be a year since we left for the ever to be remembered Chancellsorville fight. It was on the 28th April 63. How soon the year has passed away. I suppose the fight that is to come off will not be delayed a great while longer....

We have Prayer Meeting every night but Monday & that night we have Temprance meeting. So you see that our evenings are well employed.... I went to Pony Mountain last Saturday & from there we can see nearly all of our Army & also see over into Rebeldom. The sight is a grand one....

Your devoted husband,

Before beginning their march to the sea, Federal forces rip up the railroads leading into Atlanta. To make sure the lines were not rebuilt, soldiers heated the tracks in bonfires, then twisted them into "Sherman's neckties."

"**W**ar is cruelty and you cannot refine it," Sherman said in his uncompromising way, then set out to prove it. In mid-November, he and his army of 60,000 left a smoldering Atlanta behind and began their infamous march to the sea. The men had a lean 20-days' rations with them, but that was part of Sherman's total-war philosophy. "I can make the march, and make Georgia howl," he said, intending to wreak such destruction that the South would at

last see no recourse but surrender.

Dividing his army into two loosely formed wings, he sent it forth with orders to "forage liberally on the country." The foraging quickly became pillaging and sometimes wanton destruction, but "Uncle Billy" made little attempt to rein in his men. The only resistance they met was a battalion of home-guard troops—boys under 16 and men over 60. The Yankees made short work of them.

By December 10, Sherman had Savannah in his sights, and the small Confederate force holding the city fled before him. His march to the sea was over. But his battle with history was just beginning. As one historian wrote a century later: "It is still difficult to discuss unemotionally the morality of Sherman's devastation in Georgia, and later in the Carolinas." "Terror," another declaimed, "was the basic factor in Sherman's policy."

Surrounded by his generals, Sherman stares unblinkingly ahead. Alternately praised and damned for his total-war tactics, Sherman remained convinced of their necessity.

SPRING 1864

❖ **April** Porter's Union armada is temporarily trapped by low water in the Red River.

❖ **May 4** Grant's forces cross the Rapidan and head into the Wilderness.

HEAD QUARTERS, 11TH REG., NEW JERSEY V.R.
CAMP NEAR BRANDY STATION, VA.
APRIL 28, 1864

Dear Wife,

...I am still on mercy's side of the grave. I hope ere another year passes over our heads this war may be over & I at home with my dear ones. I see by the papers that Burnside has been in Washington with his troops. Where he is going we cannot tell & we make all kinds of guesses. Grant knows & we must be content.

I have nothing new to write you. The weather is fine, a little cool but pleasant.... My health continues good. My leg pains me a good deal. It comes from riding, I suppose. I send you another picture in this letter. Your album must be nearly full....

Your devoted husband,

Trundling across the Rapidan on pontoon bridges, Grant's army heads toward the Wilderness in what would become a vicious, days-long tangle with Lee.

"Up through the trees rolled dense clouds of battle smoke, circling about the green of the pines and mingling with the white of the flowering dogwoods," a Union captain wrote. Today, the scars of the tortured fighting have healed over in the woodlands of the Wilderness.

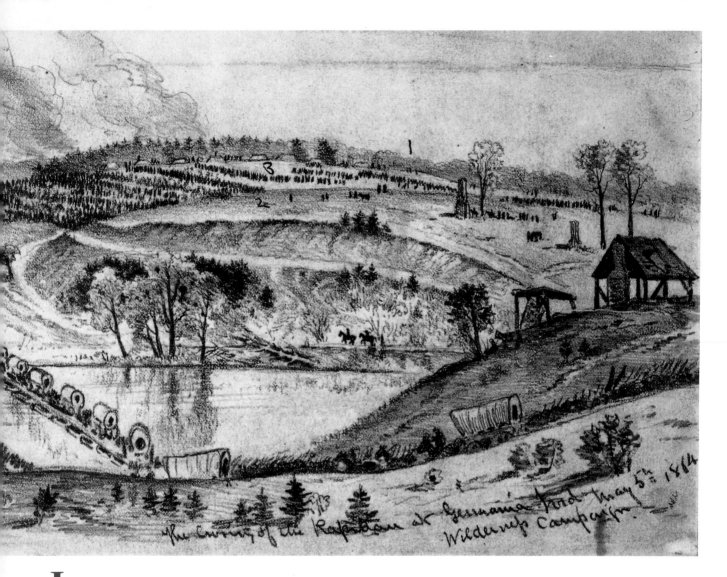

The crossing of the Rapidan at Germania Ford—May 5th 1864 Wilderness Campaign.

In early May, Lee and Grant faced off in their first direct confrontation. Their battleground was the Wilderness, the tangled thickets around Chancellorsville, where Lee had bested Hooker a year earlier. As in that encounter, Lee was vastly outnumbered, this time nearly two to one.

Well aware of Grant's strength and abilities as a general, Lee had been imploring Jefferson Davis for additional troops, writing, "We shall have to glean troops from every quarter to oppose the apparent combination of the enemy." But Lee never got his reinforcements.

On May 4, Grant's men began crossing the Rapidan River, as Lee had expected. They were on the quick march, hoping to get through the Wilderness's choked undergrowth before encountering the enemy. Anticipating the Federal movement, Lee planned to send his three corps down the three roads cutting through the Wilderness. By early afternoon the next day, fighting had erupted amid that snarled terrain. Soon the very woods flamed from the heat of battle. "All circumstances seemed to combine to make the scene one of unutterable horror. It was as though Christian men had turned to fiends, and hell itself has usurped the place of earth," a Union officer recorded. But the fight had just begun.

> **SPRING 1864**
>
> ❖ **May 5** Butler's Union Army from Fort Monroe moves up the James River toward Richmond.
>
> ❖ **May 5-6** The armies of Lee and Grant tangle in the thickets of the Wilderness.

IN THE WILDERNESS
MAY 7, 1864

Dear Wife,

I suppose you are very anxious about me as you no doubt have heard that we have been fighting. Our Regt. fought some day before yesterday & yesterday we were fighting all day. We had one of the most terriffic battles yesterday I have seen, but we fought behind Breast Works & did not lose many men. I was exausted last night & this morning at three o'clock had a hard chill. I am now at the Hospital & am some better. As we are sending the wounded back, I can send this letter.

I cannot say how things are going. I only know that we have not been whiped. We had two officers & 19 men wounded. Col. McAllister had two horses shot under him & was slightly wounded himself. I will write again as soon as I have a chance. I trust that all is well although I am fearful that things are not all right. I trust that I may come out all right, as I have so far. I recieved your...letter yesterday just before the fearful fight commenced. I am sick, tired & dirty and my hand trembles, so you will excuse this hasty scrawl as it is the best I can do. I knew you would be glad to hear from me. Love to the children & yourself....

Your loveing husband,

On the 5th we struck the enemy on the Brock road. On the 6th the fighting was terrible. At 4 o'clock in the afternoon Lee massed his forces and tried to break the center; but it was of no use, as our boys were behind works. We punished him most terribly. Many of our men shot over 100 rounds of ammunition apiece.

FROM A LETTER BY THOMAS J. HALSEY IN *HISTORY OF MORRIS COUNTY*

As the thickets of the Wilderness ignite, Union men improvise a stretcher for carting the wounded away from the flames. Those who didn't make it out faced a hideous death by fire, the cartridges in their pockets exploding in the holocaust.

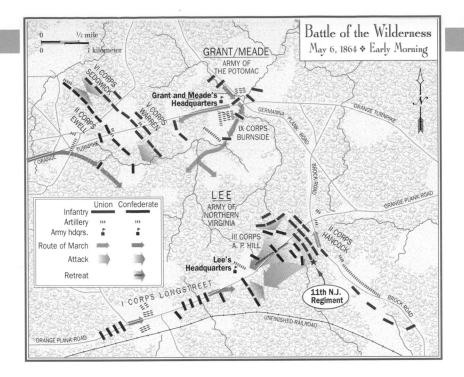

Battle of the Wilderness
May 6, 1864 ❖ Early Morning

GRANT/MEADE
ARMY OF THE POTOMAC

Grant and Meade's Headquarters

VI CORPS SEDGWICK

V CORPS WARREN

II CORPS EWELL

IX CORPS BURNSIDE

GERMANNA PLANK ROAD

ORANGE TURNPIKE

ORANGE TURNPIKE

ORANGE PLANK ROAD

BROCK ROAD

LEE
ARMY OF NORTHERN VIRGINIA

III CORPS A. P. HILL

Lee's Headquarters

II CORPS HANCOCK

11th N.J. Regiment

I CORPS LONGSTREET

UNFINISHED RAILROAD

BROCK ROAD

ORANGE PLANK ROAD

½ mile
1 kilometer

	Union	Confederate
Infantry		
Artillery		
Army hdqrs.		
Route of March		
Attack		
Retreat		

Into the evening of May 5, the two armies roared at one another in a patchwork of battle that spread across the spring-green countryside. By nightfall, neither side held a commanding advantage. Lee anxiously awaited some sign of Longstreet, whose corps—a third of Lee's army—had been marching up from Gordonsville, 30 miles to the southwest. Grant, too, had been watching, and when the Confederate reinforcements failed to appear, Grant ordered a general attack for dawn the next day.

By early morning the Yankees were shoving the Rebel line rapidly back. But the Wilderness ensnared the Union forces in its tangle, slowing and disorienting them. At this critical juncture, Longstreet's corps at last arrived. "What brigade is this?" Lee asked Brig. Gen. John Gregg. "The Texas Brigade," he replied. "Hurrah for Texas," Lee exclaimed, "Texans always move them." Wheeling into the line, he seemed about to lead the attack until the men shouted him to safety in the rear. Longstreet's corps quickly turned the tide of the battle—but only briefly. In the afternoon, Longstreet was wounded. Though he survived, 18,000 Federal soldiers and 7,800 Confederates did not.

At day's end, Grant was undeterred. "If you see the President," he told a war correspondent, "tell him, from me, that whatever happens, there will be no turning back."

Woods of the Wilderness —

SPRING 1864

❖ **Early May** Sherman begins to move his army toward Atlanta.

❖ **May 8-21** After the Battle of the Wilderness, Lee and Grant engage again at nearby Spotsylvania.

❖ **Mid-May** The Union's Red River Campaign comes to an end.

BIVOUAC ON THE PAMUNKEY 15 MILES FROM RICHMOND
SUNDAY, MAY 29, 1864

Dear Wife,

...We are fighting our way to Richmond, and this time in earnest & if Providence favors our cause we shall go there this time. Genl. Grant is the man of the times. The Army is in good spirits, although tired out with fighting, digging & marching. I know how anxious you have been about me & have written you as often as I could. I shall send this by a Major that is going home, whose time is out. I wish I was going home with him.

I have been sick now 3 weeks, dragging along with the Army. I have been in but one fight since the Battle of the Wilderness.... I have got very thin & you would hardly know me. I look so mean and dirty....

Your loving husband,

With the Wilderness smoldering behind it, Grant's army (top) hurries through the night toward its encounter with Lee at Spotsylvania. There, W. S. Hancock's corps struck a hemorrhaging blow to the Confederate line (opposite). As rain drenched the battlefield, the fallen suffocated in knee-deep mud. At right, Hancock poses, surrounded by his division commanders. Writing from Spotsylvania, Grant assured Washington that he would "fight it out on this line if it takes all summer."

True to his word, Grant did not disengage after the Battle of the Wilderness. Instead of moving north, he ordered a night march on May 7 toward Spotsylvania Court House, 12 miles deeper into Rebel territory.

Once again, Lee anticipated Grant and hurried two divisions toward Spotsylvania that same night. In the early morning light, the battle-weary Union forces neared Spotsylvania, only to find that the Confederates had beaten them there. Resuming the fight, the Union found itself unable to budge the Confederate line, until a brilliant young West Pointer, Col. Emory Upton, stepped forward with a novel strategy: Aim one blow against the "Mule Shoe," a salient on the enemy line, then pour in at the break. Though the planned attack failed, Grant was impressed enough with its results to try it again, with more concentrated force.

At first light on a rainy May 12, 15,000 Federals ramrodded the unsuspecting Confederate line and broke it. For 20 hours, the two armies battled in knee-deep mud at the infamous Bloody Angle, "a boiling, bubbling and hissing cauldron of death."

Once again the carnage—some 10,000 killed, wounded, or captured on each side—brought no immediate victor. But it did bring Grant closer to his goal—the destruction of Lee's army.

SPRING 1864

❖ **Late May** Lee takes up a defensive position on the North Anna River.

❖ **May 28** Forces of Grant and Lee skirmish along Tototomoy Creek.

❖ **May 31** Dissident Republicans meeting in Cleveland nominate John C. Frémont for president.

HEAD-QUARTERS, 11TH REGT., NEW JERSEY V.R.
CAMP AT BARKERS MILL, VA.
JUNE 7, 1864

My Dear Wife,

...I am now on duty although I am not well, but as every one is ill here in this most trying time of our country, I feel that I ought to be at my post.... With the blessing of God we mean to whip Lee or perish in the attempt....

We made a charge...under a terrific shower of shells. It was very warm & we had to travel fast. We had a long bridge to go over & the enemy had a musket battery trained on the bridge. I fell exhausted after crossing. I laid there some time & rested & then went on & took it slowly & let the shells fly as I was, as the Boys say, played out. I went on untill I reached the position where the Brigade was posted & laid down completely used up....

We are hard at work night & day.... The Army of the Potomac never knew what work was untill now. It has done more fighting, more marching & more dying in the same time than any other Army ever did in the world, I think.... But, oh, how I wish the contest might end. It is dreadful and when I think of the many thousands that are yet to be killed & wounded it makes me shudder....

We are now on McClellan's old battle fields. Our Brigade is on the extreme left of the Army...& the booming of our guns can be heard in Richmond.... Lib, if I live to get home, I shall have a great deal to talk about of this campaign....

Your affectionate husband,

While Grant did not, in fact, "fight it out...all summer" on the Spotsylvania line, he did continue his Overland Campaign, pursuing Lee south toward Richmond. Through the rest of May, the two armies vied for position, and in the skirmishing, Lee lost yet another critical player—Jeb Stuart, his cavalry commander and "the eyes and ears" of the Army.

In early June, Grant made a decisive move near the vital crossroads of Cold Harbor, where five roads and both armies had converged. After hitting the Confederate line on June 1 with a preliminary attack, Grant planned a massive assault, which was delayed by rain until June 3. That gave the Confederates a day to continue digging an elaborate "maze and labyrinth of works within works." Many Union men, meanwhile, prepared for battle by sewing labels with their names and addresses to their uniforms, sure that death awaited them. They were

right. At 4:30 a.m. 60,000 Federal soldiers attacked. Within several hours, 7,000 of them had fallen in one of the bloodiest charges of the war. The action cost Grant the respect of his men. Emory Upton, who had performed so well at the Wilderness, wrote home that he was "disgusted with the generalship.... Our men have...been foolishly and wantonly sacrificed." But Grant was not done. Lee could have Cold Harbor; he would take Petersburg.

Gun smoke envelops Union soldiers firing across no-man's-land at Cold Harbor, ten miles from Richmond. To protect themselves against overwhelming odds, Lee's men dug "intricate, zigzagged lines within lines" here at Cold Harbor. Grant's charge against those entrenchments cost him thousands of men—and a crisis in his army's confidence. Some two weeks later his men shied away from a full-scale assault on Petersburg's earthworks. In the Virginia countryside, a tidy national cemetery (left) now memorializes the Cold Harbor carnage.

SUMMER 1864

❖ **June 1-3** Grant suffers horrific losses at the Battle of Cold Harbor.

❖ **Mid-June** Grant's army crosses the James to Petersburg. Siege begins.

❖ **June 27** Sherman's forces are beaten by Johnston's at the Battle of Kennesaw Mountain, but the Union Army continues its drive toward Atlanta.

Dear Wife,

I am still alive to date. We have had some hard fighting here. Our Rgt. went in on the...16th at 5 pm. Commenced fighting at six. Fought hard untill 12 o'clock & then at intervals untill...daylight. When we were called in we had one Captain & some 5 or six privates killed and 40 wounded, many of them severly. Wm. Minton from Dover severly wounded. Our Rgt. is...nearly used up. We have now about 130 men for duty. I am in command. Col. McA commands a Brigade, Col. Schoonover half of a Brigade, which leaves me in command of our boys. C. F. Gage is with us & if we live to get through this fight will be made a Captain. He is brave as a lion & the Col. thinks a great deal of him. We are now in a strong position & I hope we may succeed in whipping the Enemy here. They fight with desperate energy.

We are now in a fine county but, oh, what devastation we make. Houses are all deserted & crops are all left to be trampled under & few our horses. I have seen but one man at work since we left Brandy Station. There is not much but corn raised here & that is not cared for as I presume they have no one to do it.... We have been shelling Petersburg now for two days. I suppose it must be deserted.

Lib, this is a fearful fight we are in & the prospect of getting out unharmed is slim. Our officers have to expose themselves and a great many of them get killed & wounded. I hope & trust I may get out all right....

Your loveing husband,

During the siege, both sides hunkered down in labyrinthine earthworks like Fort Sedgwick, whose designer, Maj. Washington Roebling, later created the Brooklyn Bridge. At right, the seven-and-a-half-ton "Dictator" ranked as the largest Federal gun pounding Petersburg.

Charles F. Gage, Halsey's friend and war comrade, eventually became his business partner.

Grant moved on Petersburg skillfully, keeping Lee confused with diversionary movements. A major Southern rail and river hub, it lay just 23 miles south of Richmond. By mid-June Federal troops were crossing the James on a 2,100-foot pontoon bridge—one of the longest ever constructed—and heading for the city. Grant's move caught Lee by surprise, but Lee knew its outcome. In late May, Lee had said, "We must destroy this army of Grant's before it gets to the James River. If he gets there it will become a siege, and then it will be a mere question of time."

Though Petersburg was defended by only a small force when the Union forces arrived, the bluecoats were daunted by its bristling breastworks and trenches. Working against time, Lee reinforced the city. Grant, knowing time and patience were his best weapons, settled into a siege.

When spring arrived, Lee knew he had to pull out from Petersburg or be destroyed. Hoping he could unite his forces with Joe Johnston's in the Carolinas, he began to move. But the odds against the South were now overwhelming. On April 1, the Confederate right wing collapsed at the Battle of Five Forks, 17 miles southwest of Petersburg. A day later, the gallant A. P. Hill was killed. "He is at rest now," Lee murmured, "and we who are left are the ones to suffer."

SUMMER 1864

❖ **Early July** Jubal Early's forces detach from Lee and move into Maryland, to distract Grant. After winning at Monocacy, Early moves on Washington and threatens its perimeter before being repulsed.

❖ **July 30** Union suffers high casualties at Petersburg's Battle of the Crater.

CHARLESTON S.C. JULY 31, 1864
CONFEDERATE STATES OF AMERICA

My Dear Wife,

...I presume they reported me from the Regt. as missing. I can immagine in a measure your feelings when you recd. the news, but a kind Providence has thus far spared my life & I trust that it will not be many months before there will be some arrangement made so that we may be exchanged....

I want you to write me & let me know how you are getting along. Have you heard from the Regt. lately?... Send your letter unsealed & write nothing but business matters....

COLUMBIA, S.C.
OCTOBER 13, 1864

Having an opportunity to send a few lines by Major Mattox who has been exchanged, I embrace the opportunity. In the first place, I am well. I presume you see by the papers that the Yellow Fever was in Charleston & so it was they removed us to this place one week ago to day. There were some few of the Officers died with it....

Your affectionate and loveing husband,

Captured in Petersburg, Halsey was taken to Richmond's Libby Prison, then moved to South

Carolina. He spent time in Columbia's Camp Sorghum (top) and Asylum Camp (bottom).

Major Halsey's release from prison would be seven months in coming, because the few prisoner exchanges made in 1864 were done on a personally arranged, one-for-one basis. In the spring of that year, Grant had halted general prisoner exchanges, in part because the South refused to acknowledge the rights of captured black soldiers to be exchanged and in part because paroled Southern prisoners often returned to the fight. "If we release or exchange prisoners captured," Grant contended, "it simply becomes a war of extermination." While Grant's action succeeded in depriving the South of vital manpower, it also kept Union soldiers imprisoned under horrific conditions.

Halsey and his fellow inmates in Columbia apparently fared far better than most. "Though our treatment was little less than that of brutes," one Columbia prisoner recalled, "still we were not reduced to the suffering and disgusting extremities which characterized the prisoners of war elsewhere." In Columbia the men were allowed to buy food from sutlers and make shelters from gathered wood. Prisoners elsewhere suffered from overcrowding, exposure to heat or cold, disease, fetid water, and lack of food. Men learned to subsist however they could. One survivor ruefully recalled, "Five chews of tobacco would buy a rat, a rat would buy five chews of tobacco."

SUMMER 1864

❖ **August 5** Farragut's forces are victorious at the Battle of Mobile Bay.

❖ **August 7** Gen. Philip Sheridan takes command of troops in Virginia's Shenandoah Valley.

❖ **September 2** Sherman enters Atlanta after Confederate troops evacuate.

COLUMBIA S.C.
FEBRUARY 10, 1865

Dear Wife,

...There are to be a few special exchanges...& an Austrian Count that is an officer in one of our N. J. Regts. has promised to take a letter for me.... As it will not go through Rebel hands, I can write what I could not when they read the letters.

In the first place, I am well & fat as a pig. I was taken sick the day I recd. your letter of Nov 5th & was very unwell for a week. I took severe cold from sleeping on the ground. We were moved from Camp Sorghum on the 12th December, where we had built ourselves good quarters, into the Assylum Yard in the upper part of the City & put inside of a stockade & the weather being cold we suffered a great deal. But Yankee ingenuity soon over came all obstacles & in spite of the Rebs, we are again comfortable....

Our rations consist of one pint of unboiled corn meal a day, ½ pint of rice for five days, one pint of sorghum for five days, 2 table spoonfuls of salt for 5 days & a small piece of soap. They have given us no meat since the 4th of October last. I think you will say rather hard fare for Yankees....

I see that the Peace Commission is come back with a flea in their ear. There are no terms but submission.... I was just going to write that there is no prospect for an exchange, when the news came...that we are all to be exchanged. If that is so, I shall soon be at home, if I live....

Your loveing husband,

"I am afraid God will suffer some terrible retribution to fall upon us for letting such things happen," a Confederate woman lamented on seeing Andersonville (above). But Union prisoner-of-war camps could be just as bad, as the high death rate at Chicago's Camp Douglas (below) affirmed.

Some places associated with the war seemed to resonate with a deeper and more abiding horror than others. Andersonville was one such place. A swampy hamlet in the Georgia backwoods in early 1864, the 27-acre hell confined 33,000 prisoners by August of the same year, making it the fifth largest "city" in the Confederacy and its most populated prison. The men here subsisted on unsifted cornmeal and lived in holes scratched in the ground, sheltered only by oilcloths or blankets. Lincoln, unable to finish his own meal one night for thinking of their plight, lamented, "Would to God this dinner...were with our poor prisoners at Andersonville."

Andersonville was not the only place of horror. In Richmond's notorious Libby Prison, 1,300 Union officers were crammed into six rooms of a converted warehouse. At the city's nearby Belle Isle prison, 90 percent of the survivors at war's end weighed under a hundred pounds.

It was the North's Camp Douglas, in Chicago, that recorded the highest mortality rate in a single month: During February 1863, 10 percent of its population—387 men—died. In all, 25,976 Confederates died in Northern prisons and 30,218 Union soldiers in Southern ones. But as poet Walt Whitman observed, "The dead...are not to be pitied as much as some of the living that have come from there...and will never recuperate."

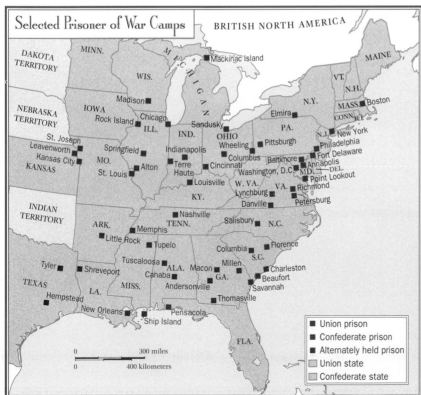

Selected Prisoner of War Camps

BRITISH NORTH AMERICA

- ■ Union prison
- ■ Confederate prison
- ■ Alternately held prison
- ▢ Union state
- ▢ Confederate state

0   300 miles
0   400 kilometers

WINTER 1865

❖ **January 31** Congress passes the 13th Amendment, abolishing slavery.

❖ **February 3** Lincoln, Seward, and Confederate envoys meet in Hampton Roads to discuss possible peace terms.

❖ **February 6** Lee is officially named commander of Confederate forces.

Lincoln spent the last half of 1864 fighting his own battle for political survival. With no conclusion to the war in sight, he faced a disgruntled electorate in his presidential campaign. No incumbent had been reelected since 1832, and his own popularity was far from assured. In July, Jubal Early added to Lincoln's vexations by threatening the very borders of the capital, coming within five miles of the White House before being driven off. Lincoln himself had gone out to Fort Stevens to watch the action, and a young soldier there, Oliver Wendell Holmes, Jr., had yelled at the gangly, unrecognized civilian to "get down before you get shot." Early ultimately was driven off, but his brashness proved one more humiliation for the administration.

In August Lincoln wrote a "blind memorandum" to his cabinet. Asking that they sign but not read it, he confessed, "It seems exceedingly probable that this Administration will not be re-elected...." Running against Lincoln was his former general, the popular George B. McClellan. The Democrats' platform, adopted in late August, called for "immediate efforts to be made for the cessation of hostilities" and seemed to hint that preservation of the Union might no longer be worth the bloodshed.

McClellan, within days, would recant the platform, as the North's fortunes in war began a dramatic reversal. On September 2, Sherman's army marched into Atlanta, ousting the South's new commander in this theater, John Bell Hood. But Sherman did not have long to savor his success. Hood, a brashly daring Confederate, conspired to draw Sherman out of Atlanta by marching on Tennessee and cutting off Northern supply lines between Atlanta and Chattanooga along the way. After chasing Hood for several weeks, Sherman gave up and returned to Atlanta, to prepare for his ravaging march to the sea.

Sherman's success cost McClellan dearly at the polls, and Lincoln once again emerged the victor, with a half-million majority that gave him 212 electoral votes to McClellan's 21. Adding to the sweetness of political success were the increasingly optimistic turns in the war. In Virginia's Shenandoah Valley—the South's "breadbasket"—Phil Sheridan had been on a rampage, making of it, as Grant had instructed, "a barren waste." And in late December Sherman wired Lincoln, saying, "I beg to present you, as a Christmas

"Damn the torpedoes! Full speed ahead!" Adm. David Farragut yelled during the August fight for Mobile Bay. The dueling here lasted three weeks before the Northern offensive finally succeeded.

J.O.DAVIDSON 1886

gift, the city of Savannah...."

Events continued to accelerate in the new year. At the end of January Congress at last passed the 13th Amendment, abolishing slavery. Elation filled the Capitol, and the House adjourned for the day, "in honor of this immortal and sublime event." A day later Sherman began his successful invasion of the Carolinas. Though Grant was locked in a frozen siege at Petersburg, the Union seemed on the precipice of victory. Perhaps knowing this, Jefferson Davis dispatched a message to Lincoln requesting "a conference with a view to secure peace to the two countries." Lincoln quickly accepted, "with a view of securing peace to the people of our common country." Meeting with three Confederate negotiators at Fort Monroe, Virginia, Lincoln offered concessions, notably a reimbursement to slave owners for the loss of their slaves. But the essential issue—one nation or two—remained unresolvable, and the meeting, as Lincoln put it, was over "without result." The season of war had not yet ended.

...On the morning of May 4th 1864 the grand old Army of the Potomac, under Grant, took up the line of march to find Lee and a battle.... It was a series of fights from that time on until we arrived in front of Petersburg, in which the 11th regiment was in every engagement.... On the 22nd we had a hard fight with General Birney in command (General Hancock being unwell). By some oversight there was a gap on our left, through which General Mahone brought his division, completely flanking us, capturing 1,600 prisoners, among which number I found myself. I thus remained in the sunny south until the next March, when I was exchanged. I rejoined the regiment near Appomattox, and had the extreme satisfaction of heading the regiment in the march through the city of Richmond on our way home...

FROM A LETTER BY THOMAS HALSEY IN *HISTORY OF MORRIS COUNTY*

Flag of the 11th New Jersey is now carefully stored at the New Jersey State Museum. Pride of the regiment, such flags were borne into battle by color-bearers.

On the Sunday of April 2, 1865, Jefferson Davis was attending services at St. Paul's Church when a messenger approached with a dispatch. As Davis read it, a fellow worshiper saw "a sort of gray pallor creep over his face." Lee was abandoning Petersburg, the dispatch informed him, and troops were to withdraw from Richmond.

The retreating Confederate forces set fire to tobacco warehouses and, later, to the three bridges across the James. Winds spread flames to other structures—some 900 buildings were destroyed. As the city burned, looters and unsavories took to the streets, creating "disorder, pillage, shouts, mad revelry of confusion," a newspaper editor wrote. The mayor, Joseph Mayo, went out to meet the approaching Union army and request that it "take possession" of the city "with an organized force, to preserve order and protect women and children."

The conquering army obliged, putting out fires, restoring order, and acting with consummate consideration. "It is impossible to

As Richmond burns, Confederate citizens flee the flames and the approaching Yankees. Set by the Southerners themselves and fanned by high winds, the conflagration spread "like Greek fire to every neighboring roof and cornice and gable."

SPRING 1865

❖ **March 4** Lincoln is inaugurated.

❖ **April 2** Richmond is evacuated.

❖ **April 3-8** Lee's army heads for North Carolina with Grant in pursuit.

❖ **April 9** Lee surrenders to Grant at Appomattox, Virginia.

describe the kind attentions of the Union soldiers," Mary Custis Lee later told her husband, Robert.

On April 4, Abraham Lincoln quietly entered the city with his young son, Tad. The black citizenry immediately recognized him, shouting "Hallelujah!" and the "Messiah." Some even knelt. "You are free," Lincoln told them, "free as air."

Spring at last came to Virginia again. For two years its soft green had been the harbinger of bloodshed. But now Lee was about to abandon the Virginia spring to the Union. Having lost Petersburg and Richmond, his army was making for North Carolina, trying to elude the Union forces that tailed doggedly after it. Marching to Amelia Court House, 40 miles from Petersburg, Lee's army arrived "wet, tired, and famishing," but the rations and supplies Lee had expected to find there had not arrived. Even as the Union noose tightened, his army had to devote a valuable day to foraging.

Marching west, Lee's troops managed to elude Sheridan's cavalry. But when bluecoats overtook the Confederate rear in the hills and hollows around Sailor's Creek, the Rebels crumpled. "My God," Lee exclaimed, "has the army been dissolved?"

Stumbling on toward Appomattox Station and its promise of supplies, Lee's army reached the area the night of April 8. His own camp in the woods northeast of the little settlement was no more than blankets spread on the ground. Like all else, his personal supply wagon was lost. As Lee met with his advisers, the sky around them glowed with the fires of encircling Federal troops. Grant had some 60,000 men, Lee perhaps 20,000, though rampant desertion left him unsure of the exact number. Even more disheartening, the Union had reached Appomattox before him. All hope of feeding his starving men was now lost. Still, his officers refused to abandon the cause. With little hope, Lee agreed to an attempt to break a path through the Federal line.

At dawn the Confederates made their move. For a moment, it seemed they might succeed. But the Union quickly repulsed them. "There is nothing left for me to do but to go and see General Grant," Lee said, "and I would rather die a thousand deaths."

The two generals met in the two-story brick home of Wilmer McLean, a local merchant-speculator. Grant arrived in his typical camp dress—bedraggled slouch hat, soldier's blouse, and mud-splashed boots. "I felt like anything rather than rejoicing at the downfall of a foe who had fought so long and so valiantly," he later said. Lee was resplendent in his best uniform hung with a gleaming sword and boots with gold spurs. The two men at first circumvented the painful issue of surrender, amicably discussing their time in the Mexican War. At last, Lee raised it. Grant's terms were simple: that the Confederates "lay down their arms, not to take them up again." Lee agreed,

and Grant wrote a brief document. Then, hesitantly, Lee requested a concession. Could all the men who owned horses keep them? Grant was amenable. Visibly pleased, Lee said, "This will have the best possible effect upon the men."

Outside, Lee mounted Traveller and moved through the press of Southern soldiers. "Men," he said with barely contained emotion, "we have fought through the war together. I have done the best I could for you."

On a chill gray April 12, Lee's men marched forward to surrender their arms. They were, according to Union commander Joshua Chamberlain, "thin, worn, and famished, but erect, and with eyes looking level into ours.... Was not such manhood to be welcomed back?" Chamberlain ordered his men to a "carry-arms." The Confederates returned the salute. It was, as

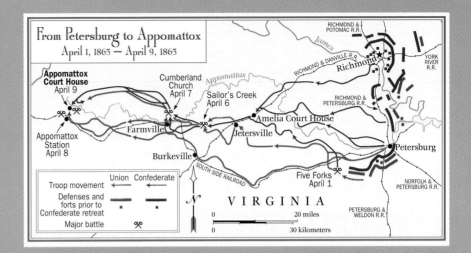

Chamberlain said, "honor answering honor."

Lee's surrender did not bring a final end to the war. In North Carolina Joe Johnston fought on, surrendering to Sherman on April 26. On June 2 the last Confederate holdouts laid down their arms. The war was over.

Old warriors—Grant, Lee, and their officers—gather at the Appomattox home of Wilmer McLean (opposite). "Our conversation grew so pleasant that I almost forgot the object of our meeting," Grant recalled. After the generals had discussed surrender, the men made their own peace, the Yankees sharing rations with the half-starved Rebs (below).

The Soldiers sharing Rations   Description on back

HD. QTRS. 11TH REGT. N.J. VOLS.
JUNE 3, 1865

Dear Wife,

I am sory you are disappointed in not seeing me home to

night. I am also disappointed as I would like to be there. I

am Division Officer of the Day and it is the last duty I expect

to do as an Officer. We expect to be mustered out to morrow

or Monday. At all event we expect to get to Trenton next week

& I am in hopes to get home, although I may not. Keep up

good spirits. It will not be long.... If there should be a review

at Trenton, would you like to come down and see it?...

I visited Mt. Vernon.... It is a pretty place. I would like to

have had you along....

I remain as ever yours,

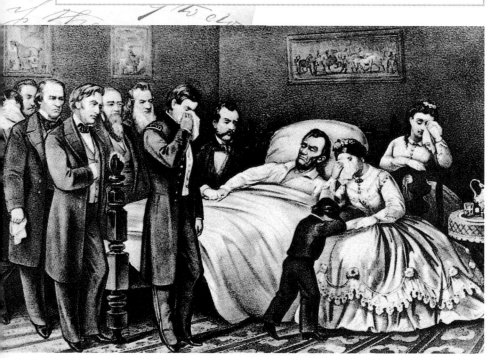

In a period illustration, Lincoln's family and compatriots gather at his deathbed after actor John Wilkes Booth shot him. Lincoln died just days after Appomattox. "He belongs to the ages," one mourner observed.

❖ The South's population at the start of the war accounted for less than half that of the divided country.

❖ Only about 10 percent of the Federal Army was older than 30, the average age at enlistment was 25. Major Halsey was 39 at war's end.

❖ The estimated total number of enlistments in the U.S. Army was 2,672,341; of that number 178,975 were black; 3,530, Native American.

Dawn light seeps among the headstones at Antietam, where 26,000 men fell in the bloodiest day of the war.

❖ Estimates for the Confederacy's total number of enlistments range between 750,000 and 1,227,890.

❖ The Union forces lost 364,000 men in the war; and the Confederate, 260,000—one out of every ten white males in the South. Some 400,000 men on both sides were wounded. Many others died from disease.

❖ The half-million foreign-born troops serving the Union included 175,000 German, 150,000 Irish, 50,000 English, and 50,000 Canadian.

❖ A total of 76 full-scale battles were fought during the war. The five bloodiest battles were Gettysburg (23,000 casualties—North; 28,100 casualties—South); Seven Days' (16,000—North; 21,000—South); Chickamauga (16,000—North; 18,500—South); Chancellorsville (17,300—North; 12,800—South); Antietam (12,400—North; 10,300—South).

❖ Eight Federal generals came from Galena, Illinois, Grant's former home.

❖ After the war, some 3,000 former Rebel officers expatriated to Brazil.

❖ Richmond's Chimborazo was the largest hospital in the world in the 1860s, with a 4,500-patient capacity.

Dear Wife,

We are having very hot weather. To day has been so hot that it was almost impossible to keep cool. I attended church at Brigade Head Qtrs for the last time. We expect to be mustered out to morrow & leave for Trenton on Tuesday morning. If we do, I shall be at home on Saturday, if all is well. I shall try hard to make it. If I have to come back to Trenton, we shall have to be paid off after we get to Trenton & I cannot tell how long we shall be there. Our papers are all ready & I am going to Army Head Qtrs in the morning to get Blanks to have the Officers Discharges made out on. I have been to see the Genl. about Capt. Gage and am in hopes that he will go home with us. I hope he will, as the Army is a bad place for young men, although the Capt. has not been led astray. But many have. Most of the Line Officers in the Regt. are hard cases.

It is now bed time & I suppose you are in bed before this time. I wonder to myself if you have been lonesome to day & wished for me home. I think you have. I think & talk about home a great deal, and am anxious to get home as I suppose you are to have me. I will write you again as soon as we get ready to start & as soon as we get to Trenton. You must excuse me for not writing oftener. I will do better from now on. Good night. Pleasant dreams. Love to the children.

I remain your loveing & affectionate husband,

Backdropped by the imposing new Capitol dome, victorious veterans from the Army of the Potomac march in the Grand Review up Pennsylvania Avenue. "The very air seemed

To men accustomed to army life and the battle-field, peace brought uncertainties. "What will become of me? Can I ever be contented again?" one cavalryman worried. Another veteran was more pragmatic. "I've killed as many of them as they have of me," he announced. "I'm going home."

For the defeated Southerners at Appomattox, the going-home process began when they received their parole—a check-like piece of paper that served as a vital passport home. But home could be hundreds of miles away. Many men made the journey on foot, only to find nothing left when they arrived. Some men devoted months, even years, to searching for loved ones who had been displaced by war. The victorious Northerners found

themselves caught in the maw of the bureaucracy at war's end. For each of the million Union men scattered across the country, a pay account had to be settled before he could be discharged. Then the new President, Andrew Johnson, ordered one final Grand Review through Washington. For two days in May, 150,000 veterans paraded down Pennsylvania Avenue, to the hurrahs of cheering crowds.

Shipped back by train to their hometowns, the returning regiments were greeted with more waving flags. After a final hometown march, they disbanded for the last time. The "strange sad war," as poet Walt Whitman had called it, was at last over.

freighted with gladness," a private recalled. Even more gladness awaited the men at homecoming. In an Arkansas scene (top), ecstatic families reunite after years of war.

SPRING 1865

❖ **April 15** Lincoln dies, and Andrew Johnson becomes President.

❖ **April 26** Lincoln's assassin is shot dead in a Virginia barn.

❖ **May 13** The final battle of the war is fought at Palmito Hill, Texas.

Healing a nation's wounds: Across the once-bloodied ground of Cemetery Ridge, veterans of the Philadelphia Brigade (left) shake hands with survivors of Pickett's division. In 1913, some 57,000 soldiers of both sides gathered here in Gettysburg for a "final demonstration that the last embers of former times have been stamped out."

After the war, the reunited nation began the slow process of healing and reintegrating itself. No longer a plurality of states, it had become a single entity. The men who had fought on both sides "knew now they had a nation, for they had seen it...touched it, climbed its mountains, crossed its rivers," historian Shelby Foote wrote. But the aftermath of war lingered on the land for almost a century. In the South, old habits and hatreds died hard, sometimes keeping progress at bay. The rest of the nation forged ahead, finishing the transcontinental railroad in 1869 and burgeoning with almost untempered industry—

and unbridled speculation. In the fall of 1873, the postwar boom ended in bust. Ulysses Grant, now President, had a new, but less straightforward, conflict on his hands as banking failures swept the country into a financial panic. A quarter of the nation's railroads succumbed to bankruptcy, and a million unemployed men wandered the land.

The veterans who had been sent home to reconstruct their lives persevered in their own fashions, living

through the postwar booms and busts as they had lived through other battles. Thomas J. Halsey returned to his family in Morris County, New Jersey, resumed his job as a railroad station agent and wood-tie purchaser, and served as a committeeman for Dover township. Sarah gave birth to two more children, and sometime in 1873 Halsey went into the lumber business with his old regimental comrade Charles Gage—the man "who was brave as a lion." It proved an inauspicious

So proud was Halsey of his service in the Union Army that he was buried in his major's uniform. Here, early in the war, he wears his captain's uniform. His cartridge case (below) still bears the scars of battle.

moment to launch a new business as it was the year of the great banking failure and financial panic. No record remains of how the business fared, only that in 1878 Jeff and Lib left the Morris County area, where both had lived most of their lives.

Moving to Holden, Missouri, they had a final child, but the little girl died before reaching her first birthday. In 1886, Halsey applied for an invalid pension, based on his war injuries. On January 20, 1893, nearly 26 years after the war's end, he died in Holden at the age of 66. Sarah survived him by a dozen years. They both rest now in Dover's Orchid Street Cemetery beside Halsey's parents and several of their own children. Halsey's fervent wish during the long days of war that a kind Providence reunite them, and that they "never...be parted again" has been granted.

Boldface indicates illustrations.
Italic indicates time line.
Note: Halsey's letters are not indexed.

● A C K N O W L E D G M E N T S

The Book Division wishes to thank the following individuals for their assistance in the preparation of the maps for this volume: Ted Alexander, Chris Bryce, Tracy D. Chernault, Troy D. Harman, Frank O'Reilly, Terrence J. Winschel.

● A D D I T I O N A L   R E A D I N G

The reader may wish to consult the *National Geographic Index* for related articles, maps, and books, including *The Blue and the Gray.* The following titles may also be of interest: Billings, John D., *Hardtack and Coffee;* Boatner, Mark M., *Civil War Dictionary;* Cornish, Dudley Taylor, *The Sable Arm: Black Troops in the Union Army, 1861-1865;* MacDonald, John, *Great Battles of the Civil War;* McPherson, James M., *Battle Cry of Freedom;* Symonds, Craig L., *A Battlefield Atlas of the Civil War;* Time Life Books, ed., *The Civil War;* Ward, Geoffrey C., *The Civil War: An Illustrated History;* Wiley, Bell Irvin, *The Common Soldier in the Civil War.*

● N O T E S   O N   C O N T R I B U T O R S

A native Virginian, **K. M. Kostyal** has often written about—and even more often contemplated—the Civil War. A longtime contributing editor to National Geographic TRAVELER, she also writes on history, travel, and culture for other publications. Though **William Halsey** has spent a lifetime as a commercial pilot, he has devoted years to historical and genealogical research. **Megan Halsey,** a graphic designer who teaches at Pratt Institute, shares her father's interest in "the Major," her great-great-grandfather.

Composition for this book by the National Geographic Society Book Division. Printed and bound by Quebecor Printing-Hawkins, New Canton, TN. Color separations by Graphic Art Service, Inc., Nashville, TN; Penn Colour Graphics, Inc., Huntingdon Valley, PA; and Phototype Color Graphics, Inc., Pennsauken, NJ.

ABBREVIATIONS: FMTW—Frank and Marie-Therese Wood, Alexandria, Virginia; NGP—National Geographic Photographer; NJSL—Bureau of Archives and History, New Jersey State Library; LC—Library of Congress; LV—The Library of Virginia: NA—National Archives; USMHI—Massachusetts Commandery Military Order of the Loyal Legion and the U.S. Army Military History Institute; (t)—top; (b)—bottom; (l)—left; (r)—right; (c)—center; (bk)—back; (f)—front.

Cover, Mark Thiessen, Courtesy of William Halsey. 1, Mark Thiessen, Courtesy of William Halsey. 2-3, The Seventh Regiment Fund, Inc. 4, Victor Boswell. 6-7, LC. 8-9, Confederate Memorial Hall, New Orleans, LA. 10-11, LC. 12-13, FMTW. 13, NA. 14-15, LC. 16, Don Troiani, Southbury, CT, from *Echoes of Glory: Arms and Equipment of the Union*, Photograph by Larry Sherer, © 1991 Time-Life Books Inc. 16-17, The Western Reserve Historical Society, Cleveland, Ohio. 18, LC. 18-19, from *Civil War: Bloodiest Day*, Photograph by Larry Sherer, © 1984 Time-Life Books Inc. 20, Sam Abell/NGP. 21, Collection of the New-York Historical Society. 22-23, USMHI. 24, (tr) American Red Cross; (bl) The Historical Society of Washington, DC; (br) LC. 25, Courtesy of Joseph Bailey. 26, (t) FMTW; (b) USMHI. 27, (t) LC; (b) LC, Photograph Courtesy of The Museum of the Confederacy, Richmond, Virginia. 28, Courtesy of the Stock Montage, Inc. 29, Sam Abell/National Geographic Image Collection. 30-31, Anne S.K. Brown Military Collection, Brown University Library. 31, (t) The William Stanley Hoole Special Collections Library, The Unviversity of Alabama; © Henry Groskinsky, Courtesy of Norman Flayderman, Fort Lauderdale, FL, from *The Civil War: Master Index*, Photography by Henry Groskinsky, © 1987 Time-Life Books Inc.; (b) Victor Boswell. 32, (c) Virginia Department of Historic Resources Photo, Courtesy of LV; (b) USMHI. 32-33, The Virginia Historical Library, Richmond, Virginia. 33, The Virginia Historical Library, Richmond, Virginia. 34, (t) LC; (bl) Courtesy of Kean Archives; (br) George Eastman House. 35, (both) NA. 36, (tl) New Jersey State Archives, Department of State; (tr) Roger D. Hunt Collection at USMHI; (bl) NJSL; (br) NJSL. 37, (tl) John Kuhl Collection; (tr) NJSL; (bl) NJSL; (br) NJSL. 38, LV. 38-39, FMTW. 39, LC. 40, Courtesy of Tim Garrett and Bill Henderson, The Picket Post, Fredricksburg, Virginia. 41, (t) Courtesy of American Heritage Picture Collection; (b) NA. 42, Stamatelos Brothers, Cambridge, MA, from *Echoes of Glory: Arms and Equipment of the Union*, Photograph by Larry Sherer, © 1991 Time-Life Books Inc. 42-43, LC. 44, FMTW. 46, Sam Abell/NGP. 48, (l) NJST; (r) The Museum of the Confederacy, Richmond, Virginia, Photography by Dennis McWaters. 49, Minnesota Historical Society. 50-51, Print Collection Miriam and Ira D. Wallach, Division of Art, Prints and Photographs, The New York Public Library, Astor, Lenox and Tildon Foundation. 52, Courtesy of Tim Garrett and Bill Henderson, The Picket Post, Fredricksburg, Virginia. 52-53, (t) Mark Thiessen, Courtesy of William Halsey; (b)

Courtesy of The Civil War Library and Museum, Philadelphia, PA, from *Echoes of Glory: Arms and Equipment of the Union*, Photograph by Larry Sherer, © 1991 Time-Life Books Inc. 53, NA. 54-56, (all) LC. 56-57, NA. 58, (l) James C. Frasca Collection; (r) Courtesy of the Atlanta Historical Center, from *Echoes of Glory: Arms and Equipment of the Confederacy*, Photograph by Larry Sherer, © 1991 Time-Life Books Inc. 59, Collection of the New-York Historical Society. 60, LC. 60-61, Chicago Historical Society, ICHi-08279, Photographer Alexander Gardner. 61-62, (both) FMTW. 62-63, Bequest of Martha C. Karolik for the M. and M. Karolik Collection of American Painting 1815-1865, Courtesy of the Museum of Fine Arts, Boston. 64, FMTW. 65, (t) FMTW; (b) LV. 66, (l) Battles and Leaders of the Civil War, Volume III; (r) LC. 66-67, LC. 68-69, (both) Courtesy of the American Heritage Picture Collection. 70, (t) Courtesy of the Illinois State Historical Library; (bl) FMTW; (br) LC. 71, (t) The Lincoln Museum, Fort Wayne, Indiana; (b) Chicago Historical Society, ICHi-11472. 72, (t) Eleanor S. Brockenbrough Library, The Museum of the Confederacy, Richmond, Virginia, Copy Photography by Katherine Wetzel; (b) FMTW. 73, (t) NA; (b) FMTW. 74, Mark Thiessen, Courtesy of William Halsey. 74-75, LC. 76, (t) *History of the Eleventh New Jersey Volunteers*, Thomas B. Marbaker, Trenton, NJ 1898; (b) FMTW. 77, (t) Sam Abell; (b) FMTW. 78, (t) LC; (c) LC; (b) FMTW. 79, (t) FMTW; (b) National Park Service. 80-81, (t) Sam Abell/NGP; (b) LC. 81, LC. 82, (bk) The Virginia Historical Society, Richmond, Virginia; (ft) LV. 83, (t) USMHI; (b) LC. 84, Joseph Bailey. 84-85, FMTW. 85, USMHI. 86, (l) Roger D. Hunt Collection at USMHI; (r) NA. 86-87, LC. 88, (both) FMTW. 89, (both) FMTW. 90, (l) FMTW; (r) Beverly M. DeBose III Collection, from *The Civil War: Sherman's March*, Photograph by Michael W. Thomas, © 1986 Time-Life Books Inc. 90-91, NA. 91, William Gladstone Collection. 92, John Kuhl Collection. 92-93, FMTW. 94, (l) LC; (r) John Kuhl Collection. 94-96, (all) LC. 96-97, Eastern National/Chickamauga and Chattanooga National Military Park. 97, FMTW. 98, (t) Don Troiani, Southbury, CT; (tc) NJSL; (bc) Eleanor S. Brockenbrough Library, The Museum of the Confederacy, Richmond, Virginia, Copy Photography by Katherine Wetzel; (b) Music Division, The New York Public Library for the Performing Arts, Astor, Lenox and Tildon Foundation. 99, (t) Chicago Historical Society; (c&b) Music Division, The New York Public Library for the Performing

Arts, Astor, Lenox, and Tildon. 100, (t) Courtesy of Christopher Nelson, from *The Civil War: Master Index*, Copied by Larry Sherer, © 1987 Time-Life Books Inc.; (b) USMHI. 101, (t) National Park Service; (b) Collection of the Newark Museum, Purchase 1944 Wallace M. Scudder Bequest Fund. 102, (l) Courtesy of the Atlanta History Center, from *Echoes of Glory: Arms and Equipment of the Confederacy*, Photograph by Larry Sherer, © 1991 Time-Life Books Inc; (r) © Henry Groskinsky, from *The Civil War: First Blood*, Photography by Henry Groskinsky, © 1983 Time-Life Books Inc. 103, (t) LC; (b) Courtesy Georgia Department of Archives and History. 104, (t) Valentine Museum, Richmond, Virginia; (c) The Museum of the Confederacy, Richmond, Virginia, Photography by Katherine Wetzel; (b) Marian B. Ralph. 105, FMTW. 106, George F. Mobley. 106-107, LC. 108, FMTW. 109, NA. 110-111, FMTW. 112, (t) Courtesy of the Historical Society of Delaware; (b) FMTW. 113, (t) FMTW; (bl) LV; (br) FMTW. 114, Sam Abell/National Geographic Image Collection. 114-115, LC. 116-117, (t) FMTW; (b) FMTW. 118-119, State Historical Society of Wisconsin. 119, FMTW. 120, (t) Washington/Custis/Lee Collection, Washington and Lee University, Lexington, Virginia; (c) Courtesy Special Collections, James G. Leyburn Library, Washington and Lee University, Lexington, Virginia; (b) Page One Publications, Richmond, Virginia. 121, (t) LC; (b) The Museum of the Confederacy, Richmond, Virginia, from *Echoes of Glory: Arms and Equipment of the Confederacy*, Photograph by Larry Sherer, © 1991 Time Life Books Inc. 122, (t) Chicago Historical Society, ICHi-10503, Photographer Bishop, Army of the Cumberland; (b) LC. 123, LC. 124, Collection of the New-York Historical Society. 124-125, NA. 126, Sam Abell/NGP. 126-129, (both) LC. 130, NA. 130-131, FMTW. 131, The Seventh Regiment Fund, Inc. 132-133, FMTW. 133, Sam Abell/NGP. 134, *History of the Eleventh New Jersey Volunteers*, Thomas B. Marbaker, Trenton, NJ 1898. 134-135, NC. 135, LC. 136-137, (both) Mark Thiessen, Courtesy of William Halsey. 138, Chicago Historical Society, ICHi-22085. 138-139, NA. 140-141, Collection of the New-York Historical Society. 142, New Jersey State Archives, Department of State. 142-143, Valentine Museum, Richmond, Virginia. 144, Tom Lovell. 145, LC. 146, FMTW. 146-147, Maria Stenzel. 148-149, (both) LC. 150, RG-25, Special Collections, Pennsylvania State Archives. 151, (t) Roger D. Hunt Collection at USMHI, (b) Mark Thiessen, Courtesy of William Halsey.

Library of Congress CP Data
Kostyal, K. M., 1951-
    Field of battle : the Civil War letters of Major Thomas J. Halsey
  / [K.M. Kostyal, author].
      p.   cm.
    Includes bibliographical references (p.   ) and index.
    ISBN 0-7922-3412-X (regular). — ISBN 0-7922-3413-8 (deluxe)
    1. United States—History—Civil War, 1861-1865—Campaigns. 2. United States—History—Civil War, 1861-1865—Pictorial works. 3. Halsey, Thomas J.—Correspondence. 4. United States—History—Civil War, 1861-1865—Personal narratives. 5. Soldiers—United States—Correspondence. I. Halsey, Thomas J. II. Title.
E470.K65 1996
973.7'81—dc20
                                           96-4192
                                         CP